ZAPOTEC DEVIANCE

Zapotec Deviance

THE CONVERGENCE OF FOLK AND MODERN SOCIOLOGY

BY HENRY A. SELBY

Foreword by Howard S. Becker

UNIVERSITY OF TEXAS PRESS, AUSTIN AND LONDON

*The publication of this book was assisted by a
grant from the Andrew W. Mellon Foundation*

Title page decoration: early jade sculpture from Zacatlan. Courtesy
of the *Handbook of Middle American Indians*, vol. 3.

Library of Congress Cataloging in Publication Data

Selby, Henry A
    Zapotec deviance; the convergence of folk and modern
sociology.

    Bibliography: p.
    1. Zapotec Indians.   2. Deviant behavior.   3. Oaxa-
ca, Mexico (State)—Social conditions.   I. Title.
F1221.Z3S44   301.6'2   73-22480
ISBN 0-292-79800-8

Printed in the United States of America
Composition by G&S Typesetters, Austin
Printing by The University of Texas Printing Division, Austin
Binding by Universal Bookbindery, Inc., San Antonio

CONTENTS

FIGURES

MAPS

FOREWORD

The sociological study of deviance, though it has occasionally borrowed exotic examples from the ethnographic literature, has been based almost entirely on Western materials, mostly from the United States. The anthropological study of deviance has relied much more on psychology and psychoanalysis than has sociology for its explanatory arguments. Both areas of study have suffered from their failure to connect. Sociology has paid the price of taking too much for granted, of identifying deviance too closely with those actions that violate the American sense of propriety and the criminal laws of the United States. Anthropology has labored to make theories of individual psychology explain collective phenomena and has failed to make the most of the theoretical leverage provided by the broad cultural variations in its ethnographies.

Henry Selby brings to his study of a traditional anthropological topic—witchcraft—a late development in sociological theory, the so-called labeling, or interactionist, theory of deviance. He brings to sociologists of deviance a number of things: a comparative non-U.S. case to add to the available evidence on deviance, a welcome addition to the slim body of detailed studies of the deviance process; an example of the usefulness, indeed, the necessity, of exploring the ethnosemantics of any area of deviance; a model study of the dynamics of labeling; and important evidence on the relation between the attributes and acts of the person and the labels that the social process attaches to him (especially the question of the validity of those labels).

The interactionist theories of deviance now popular in sociology have great promise for anthropological studies. They make it possible, as more psychologistic schemes do not, to study deviance as a form of collective social action in which the entire society and all its members are involved. Since Selby devotes a good deal of attention to this in his book, I will go on to point out the lessons that Selby's research has for sociologists.

Because sociology has typically confined itself to American materials, its theories tend to the worst kind of ethnocentrism. If deviance is a drama whose main event consists of some people in a society accusing others of having done wrong, then the subject matter of those accusations could be almost anything. We tend to think of deviance as consisting, in its essence, of whatever is condemned in our own contemporary surroundings, and thus we fatally confuse the sociological drama of accusation and the moral legitimacy of the substance of the accusation. Surely, we think, murder is *really* deviant. But Selby shows us that it is not—not in his Oaxacan village, anyway—and certainly not as deviant as the lack of humility and respect, which we might hardly notice, let alone condemn. We recognize that cultures vary in their moral codes, but we find it hard to respect the implications of that fact. The chief implication that Selby's case thrusts under our noses is that there is nothing necessary about the content of those moral accusations, and that what people are accused of may, from the perspective of another culture, not seem at all immoral. If sociologists accepted that theory, they could, for instance, stop arguing about whether imperialism and racism are *really* deviant—since so defining them is only an indirect way of condemning what should be condemned outright—and pursue the more interesting question of how people who do such immoral things manage to escape labeling and condemnation.

Sociologists will find Selby's ethnosemantic analysis worth imitating, whether or not they use the precise techniques now popular in anthropology. By exploring the entire domain in which accusations of wrongdoing or evil arise, by noting the interrelations of the concepts so elicited, and by looking for the underlying dimensions that give that domain and those concepts their logical coherence, they can avoid equating the field of deviance with what is officially condemned and criminalized, as they so often do now. They will begin to get an empirically based conception of the underlying premises on which Americans of various kinds act, by seeing what ideas can be appealed to successfully in what situations of deviance imputation. Sociologists interested in applying their knowledge will see the basis on which current labels for deviance are legitimated, and thus they will learn how to remove deviance labels from behavior they think ought to be let alone and how to attach them to behavior they want to attack.

Many sociologists who attempt a "labeling" approach to deviance do not actually study the details of the process by which deviance is imputed by some people to other people and the contingencies that govern whether those imputations succeed or fail. With this failure they betray the theory they intend to support. It is only by paying attention to that process in all its complexity that one can do justice to the importance of all the parties to the drama of deviance. No sooner does one focus solely on the results of that process (as in studying the alleged deviants alone) than he begins to ignore what the other people involved actually do and thus makes all kinds of erroneous assumptions about what has gone on. For instance, one tends to assume that others respond in a monolithically homogeneous way to the acts in question. This assumption shows up in the use of passive grammatical constructions. Authors begin to say, "Deviants are labeled and then . . ." instead of using an active construction, which would require them to say exactly who did the labeling. Though the use of passive constructions is an ingrained academic vice, their use in this area almost always indicates a failure to study the entire process and thus to know who did it; in the absence of knowledge of who did that, we necessarily have to use a passive, impersonal construction. Selby shows us the benefits of a study of the detail of the process. That detail leads him to the important finding that no two witch accusers have the same group of people in mind, a finding that could easily be duplicated in any American city (though not for witchcraft) and whose significance sociologists have, by not finding out about it, managed to ignore.

Some controversy has arisen about whether the imputations of deviance made by doctors, law-enforcement officials, teachers, and other officially accredited deviance definers are accurate. Insofar as interactionist theories make those imputations problematic and do not accept their accuracy as given, they stand as an indictment of Establishment practice and an accusation of victimization of those labeled deviant by people who are politically and professionally powerful. Sociologists sometimes provide a defense of conventional practice by doing research that purports to show that official diagnoses are pretty accurate after all. If that is so, then the potential disparity between official labels and the actual distribution of the behavior or attribute in question (as that might be discovered even by conventional means of case finding), a disparity made possible by the theoretical independence of those two matters, isn't so important after all. Oaxacan witchcraft becomes important to this argument because, like Selby, few of the social scientists who accept our own deviance-finding procedures as accurate would even admit the existence of anything to be found in the case of witchcraft. If, nevertheless, people in Selby's village can routinely discover witches who we know do not exist, it is a strong proof that the theoretical possibility can occur. Of course, because Oaxacan peasants can find witches that do not exist does not mean that physicians and policemen find lunatics and criminals where none exist. But it shows the necessity of keeping the possibility in mind and suggests the mechanism by which it can happen: one needs to find a culprit and searches among those about whom one knows little enough to make it possible to attribute to them a deviant inhumanity.

I hope I have said enough to indicate that social scientists beyond those anthropologists interested in witchcraft or Mesoamerica will find this study, with its rich, meaty data and its superb analytic reasoning, extremely rewarding. Sociologists of deviance, especially, need to add Selby's findings and analyses to that fund of fully researched cases from which we all work.

HOWARD S. BECKER
Northwestern University

PREFACE

I first went to the Oaxaca Valley in 1965 with my wife and two children. I had had some previous experience in Mexico, having done some field work with Hugo Nutini in the summer of 1964, but this was the first time I was on my own. Since Oaxaca is a tourist center, there was not one house to be found that could be rented, and so we were forced to look in the small towns around Oaxaca to see if we could get something. We went to a market town near the city and rented the house of a man who was to become my guardian angel and very good friend, Sr. Aurelio Bautista. He was interested in social anthropology and in students. He was a peasant farmer who had sent three of his sons through the university. He took me on a tour of the valley to village communities that fit my specifications: they had to be traditional and lack cash cropping and small industries. I was determined to get an unwesternized village community where I could carry out my study. He found one and also found that it was closed to outsiders. For a month he worked with the town officials while I fretted; finally, we gained entry. On what turned out to be our final trip together to the village, he managed to elicit from me exactly what I wanted to study, and when I explained about deviance, he suggested that I would want to look into witchcraft. I told him that I wasn't interested in witchcraft; that was a traditional anthropological topic, and I wanted to do work that would be contemporary, bearing on problems that we were grappling with today. He said nothing but waited, and six months later I was asking him all the questions I could think of about witchcraft. He proceeded, as he always has, to help me to the greatest degree possible. He was the first in a long line of benefactors who have made this book possible.

Many people have indulged me during the writing of this book. First, my thanks must go to Nevitt Sanford, who was director of the Institute for the Study of Human Problems and who not only supported me financially through graduate school but also had enough faith in me to allow me free rein. Bernard Siegel introduced me to field work with the Tiwa Indians of the American Southwest and encouraged me throughout my graduate career. A. Kimball Romney and Roy G. D'Andrade provided a stimulus in my graduate years that made that trying experience thoroughly worthwhile. Benjamin D. Paul read the dissertation that I wrote in 1966 and made many helpful suggestions, not the least of which was one to Howard Becker, that something might be made of all this and that perhaps Becker could get me to do more research and to write it up. He did, and I did, and this is the outcome. I do not think that many editors have the patience and skill of Howard S. Becker, and it is certainly not too much to say that most of the virtues of this book stem from his encouragement and candor. Not only does he believe in doing good anthropology-sociology, but also he believes in writing well, and his efforts in editing this manuscript, which he has followed from its prenatal stages up to postadolescence, have been magnificent.

There have been many people whom I have consulted and belabored during the writing. John Hotchkiss has been my constant companion in the field since 1965. Among my friends and colleagues who have lent their time to criticize and help, I would like to thank Ira Buchler, Richard Bauman, Douglas Uzzell, Bruce Hupp, and Ayse Sertel. Fredda White has typed and retyped this manuscript, and I want to thank her very much for her painstaking help.

My greatest debt of gratitude is owed to three families. My own family was a constant source of support and encouragement, even when things were looking very glum and I was reacting according- ly. My children became village children, my wife became an anthro- pologist, and we all became devoted to the people of the com- munity where we were subsequently to return year after year. My wife has not only put up with temperament, but has also insisted on decent prose and accurate ethnography. She has carefully read this book and argued many of the points with me. I would like to dedicate the book to two Mexican families: the family of Aurelio Bautista and the family of Zeferino Galindo, with whom we stayed during our first two years in the village. The village itself remains anonymous, which is as it must be, since the villagers took me into their confidence. Pseudonyms are used throughout the text, and even though several names are actually found in the community, none correspond to the person.

Field work for this study was carried out in the years 1965–1971. There were four periods during which I worked and lived in the community: January to December 1965; July to August 1966; June to August 1967; and July to August 1968. In 1965 and 1966 my wife was present in the village; four other field workers, Frances Macaleavey, Linda Swartz, Michael Mackinlay, and Richard Gold- berg, have also spent short periods of two to four months working there on related problems. In the field-work periods from 1965 to 1968 I lived in the community, but the writing was completed in Oaxaca City.

The first year was spent in collecting data for the initial stages of the study. For eight months I collected Zapotec texts and did the preliminary analysis, while carrying out the essential tasks of

census, basic ethnographic survey, and genealogical work. Two
complete censuses of the village were collected in March and December of 1965. Genealogical work was carried out by Mackinlay
and myself in 1965 and 1966. The initial findings on the process
of labeling a witch were presented in my Ph.D. dissertation (Selby,
1966). In the summer of 1966, one further month was spent in
the intensive collection of textual materials on the categories of
deviance. The texts were further analyzed, and a total of 121 items
that had been elicited from nine informants over a period of nine
months as properly belonging to the domain of "deviant person"
(čaab mo' ten) were collated and submitted to three local judges
for a judgment-of-differences task. Forty-four distinguishable categories of deviance remained; in cases where any one of the judges
deemed that a statement was redundant in the corpus, it was not
retained.

A rating-and-ranking test was carried out with these statements
(along with two test items on good behavior, which were used as
a check to ensure that the informants understood the task). Thirty
informants were then contacted and these forty-four items were
rated on a five-point scale. The points on the scale were labeled in
Zapotec and coincided with locally salient discriminations: "very
evil," "medium evil," "evil, but a little, that's all," "neither good
nor evil [an unimportant thing]," and "good, in general." After
I read the items in Zapotec to each informant three times, the rating task commenced. Twenty-three informants were able to complete this half of the sorting task. Then, each class was taken and
rank ordered. All the items that had been assigned to the "very
evil" category were rank ordered; next, those that had been assigned to the "medium evil," and so on. Ties were permitted. Items
judged to be "not applicable" (i.e., neither good nor evil) were assigned a tied rank at the bottom of the rankings.

Sampling techniques were not used. It was simply absurd in this
situation to expect that any informant picked at random could or

would do the task. The items were sensitive ones, and the task was arduous and demanded long periods of concentration. The entire task was completed in one session in order to avoid as much "noise" in the data as possible. Sessions lasted from one to four hours, modally for two and one-half. I made an attempt to select men and women in equal proportions (the women generally proving more difficult to convince that they *could* complete the task), and approximately equal numbers of men and women, and people over and under age forty, completed the task. Twenty-one subjects participated fully.

In 1967 and 1968 interviews were carried out with six informants. These informants are identified by pseudonyms in the text. Eusebia, a young married woman with four children, was interviewed for about 150 hours. Amelia, a woman of sixty years of age, was interviewed for about 80 hours. Jesús, a man of thirty-five years of age, was interviewed both in the community and in my house in the United States for about 100 hours. Santos, a man thirty years old, was interviewed in the community for about 180 hours. Javier, an older man of seventy, was interviewed for about 45 hours; and Jorge, twenty-eight years old, was interviewed for only 25 hours. Interviews were all conducted in the same manner. Eliciting a text in Zapotec that explicated the item in question, I then asked about each phrase in the text (most frequently, "Give me an example of '————' "). Points that remained obscure were noted and either explicated more fully or left for another informant at another time. Before interviewing Jesús and Amelia, I made a collation of the materials in the form of a rough draft of this manuscript, and points that remained unclear were more fully explored with both (particularly the items on witchcraft and sexual activity). Finally, the whole text was checked by Jesús in the United States; errors of fact were noted and appropriate corrections made. By the time the final interviews were being completed, I realized that the same materials were coming up, over and over again, and that my pa-

tience and interest were beginning to flag; the point of diminishing
returns had been reached. The number of hours of interviews, it
might be noted, are very conservatively estimated. I carried on informal interviewing with a wider population at all times, and at
least twenty persons contributed to the explication of the items on
deviant behavior. Although formal interviews were carried on
during the day, much invaluable material (particularly that dealing
with supernaturally linked phenomena) was collected at night,
while I sat in the porchway of the house, chatting with the family
I lived with and with visitors. Because of the impact of social
geography on the study (as will be seen in the chapters on witchcraft), I selected a different house in 1967 and 1968, taking care
to ensure that informants from all parts of the village were consulted.

Doing anthropology is a collaborative effort, more so than any
other form of social research. I was lucky, as every anthropologist
must be, in finding people of talent and imagination who were willing to become informants and thus step outside their role to help
me. This book represents the best we could do. It is a privilege to
work in a traditional community. And, despite the fact that I have
chosen to write about the negative side of their lives, I hope that I
have been able to convey my admiration for the villagers' integrity,
complexity, intelligence, and contemporaneity. They may live in a
world different from our own, but in every important human way
they are much as we are, and I hope that I have been able to convey
this similarity through their speech and their thoughts.

ZAPOTEC DEVIANCE

1. The Study of Deviance

The subject is deviance: conceptions of deviant behavior and their correlates in a traditional Mesoamerican community in the Oaxaca Valley of Mexico. The village where I worked for six years seems, on first acquaintance, an unlikely place to carry out such a study. Life seems tranquil and orderly, at least on the surface. The villagers say repeatedly, and with some justification, "We are all humble men," adding that humility is not a way of life in all the valley communities; "This village is different from other villages, because here you can walk the streets without worrying, because the people here get along well, not like the other villages, which are plagued by factional disputes." True, there was a Protestant minister who came proselytizing in 1955 and did manage to bring about divisions and factionalism in the community (one man was accidentally killed), but all that has died down now. There is no Protestant pastor in the community the way there was in the fifties, and interest in a new religion has subsided. True, there are killings from time to time, but they aren't "murder" in the sense of killing one's own people, without justification. There have been four killings between the village and its rival-neighbor in the last ten years, the last a dramatic feud in which "guns" were hired, adultery was involved, and an entire family was wiped out. But one does not have to feel that the community morals were involved, since the killings took place between (and not within) villages and therefore did not infringe upon the moral canons that bind community conduct. True, also, there was a witch killing in 1960, but no one can be really sure if it was a justified killing or not, and the incident has been swept under the rug.

By and large it is a peaceful community, and it was chosen for that reason. Anthropologists always have to study what is in their subjects' minds, and the last thing I wanted was some kind of fixation on a particular kind of deviance (factionalism, for example, or murder) that would dominate the data.

Second, it is a traditional community, economically unchanged since the Spanish conquest when domestic animals, as well as wheat and steel-tipped plows, were added to the local inventory. Zapotec is spoken routinely in the home and is the first language learned by children. The traditional costume is still worn by the women and is one of the twenty-odd distinctive costumes of Oaxaca (Cordry and Cordry, 1968:270–272). The villagers still have those elegantly tailored manners that we might aspire to, but never achieve: the soft-spoken manner, the ritual greetings, the enormous care not to offend, the specially groomed vocal inflections to indicate every shade of respect, the kissing of hands, and, above all, the gravity of manner that marks a man of respect. But things are changing. Jesús complains that the children have no respect or manners any more and that it is impossible to teach them because they listen too much to the schoolteachers. ("They don't even know how to say 'hello' to their godfathers any more," he protests.) I wanted a traditional community because I didn't see the point of carrying out a study of values or deviance in the anthropological

manner in a community that was highly hispanicized and where
the villagers could cite the civil code. One gives up a lot in the
way of intelligibility—one has to work in Zapotec, and Zapotec is
an extremely difficult language; I am familiar with my Zapotec
texts, but I do not speak the language. One also gives up a lot of
interpretability (as I found writing this book), because, unlike
people who write about deviance in Western society, and particularly in the United States, I cannot play upon those ironies of contrast between the "straight" and the "deviant" worlds that enliven
and inform the writings on deviance at home. One may have Goff-
manesque insights about the management of self in Zapotec, but
trying to communicate these is a cumbersome business. Whatever
one gives up, however, one gains by forcing one's self to chart a
really new world. If this experiment is a success, or if it broadens
our minds about the nature of deviance, then such success is owed
to the fact that the study was carried out in such an out-of-the-way
place.

Let me introduce the discussion that follows by talking about the
modern theory of deviant behavior. One of the things that I discovered about the Zapotecs is that they have applied the modern
theory of deviance to their thinking about, and their response to,
deviance; as a consequence, this book is a utopian case study. It
describes how a community operates when our most advanced
knowledge of crime and criminology is put to use. I believe that
much of the world operates this way (particularly, people who live
in small-scale communities) and that our rediscovery of the nature
of deviance is an index of our alienation from the cultural conditions of living that have characterized human communities since
they were first formed. Or, if this is too strong, it is fair to say that
urbanization, industrialization, and the invention of highly complex
and interdependent forms of society have obscured the basic social
conditions that give rise to deviant behavior to such a degree that

we have had to reinvent a theory that was plain common sense for the people who lived in small-scale communities, as all people did until the relatively recent past.

In Western social science three kinds of explanations have been adduced to explain deviant phenomena: biological, psychological, and social psychological. Biological theories reappear from time to time (most recently in the form of a chromosomal hypothesis that became popular with the discovery that the Boston Strangler had an extra male chromosome, i.e., he was XYY instead of XY), but they usually die after an initial vogue for reasons that will become clear below.[1]

The most natural, commonsensical explanation for deviant behavior (for us) lies in psychological or social psychological explanations. We habitually explain human conduct in psychological terms, so it seems natural that, if you are going to ask the question "why do people go wrong?" and think that it is an answerable question as posed, you will seek a psychological explanation. The Zapotecs (and modern research) can disabuse us of this type of explanation, but the idea dies hard. Attempts to differentiate between criminals and noncriminals on psychological grounds have been made in the past, but without much success. Studies were carried out with institutionalized populations with or without matched controls, and attempts were made to analyze the differences in personality between criminals and noncriminals in the hope of predicting or accounting for criminal behavior. The Gluecks (1956), for example, compared 500 correctional school inmates with 500 nondelinquent boys matched for residential area, age, ethnic origin, and intelligence rating, but they found that the groups differed only to a modest degree in conspicuous mental pathology, indicating that delinquency can be attributed to mental or emotional disturbances

[1] For a recent discussion of the data that favor the chromosomal hypothesis, see Court-Brown and Smith (1969).

only in a small proportion of cases. As early as 1950, Schuessler and Cressey (1950), after reviewing 133 studies of criminal personality, decided that there was no way to predict criminality from personality data and that the overlap on all personality traits was simply too great. Deviants in this statistical sense were indistinguishable from the general population. Similarly, efforts to locate a personality type that will predict (or postdict) a specific pattern of deviance (the "alcoholic personality," for example) have largely been abandoned.

As we all know, much work has been carried out and is still being done to formulate a social psychological theory of criminality. Although it will be conceded that there is no specific personality constellation that predicts criminal behavior, many care to examine the sociocultural conditions underlying "inflated crime rates," or other forms of deviance. The studies vary in scope and theoretical interests, from the highly psychodynamic to the sociological and the ecological. At the psychological end of the continuum, interest focuses on the social conditions that bring about personality conflicts or on psychological configurations that can plausibly be linked to a future deviant career. In some of the more ambitious studies, the attempt is made to predict deviance or crime "in general," but more often the focus is selective, and a particular type of deviance is seen to be more probable because of a particular personality style. The McCords' studies (McCord and McCord, 1959, 1960) are good illustrations. In their treatment of the causes of crime, which they derived from an analysis of the lives of 253 subjects whose childhoods and adolescences had been studied in the Cambridge-Somerville project, they came to the conclusion that intelligence was not related to crime, nor was physique, and that neighborhood by itself was not sufficient to produce crime. Home atmosphere was related (broken homes and quarrelsome-but-affectionate homes being positively correlated); so were parental discipline (lax or erratic discipline was positively correlated), father's

personality (paternal absence, cruelty, or neglect being positively
correlated), and, most important of all, mother's personality (ma-
ternal passivity, cruelty, and absence being positively correlated).
In their study of children who turned out to be alcoholics from
that same population, they concluded that alcoholism originated in
the male's incapacity to meet culturally defined role demands because of his intense dependency needs arising from a general stress
and inadequate nurture in childhood.

At the more sociological end we have studies of social class and
deviance, or of the "culture of poverty," and here the results are
usually predictable—the lower the class, the higher the incidence
of deviant behavior. Hollingshead (1958) finds that the lowest
class of a five-class system has a psychosis rate that is four times
greater than the upper classes for certain ages. There is a greater
incidence of delinquency in lower social classes, and adult crime is
higher in lower-class areas (Morris, 1957; Reiss and Rhodes,
1961). Finally, an omnibus theory of the genesis of deviance derived from the arrangements of the social structure has been developed by Merton (1957).

One major problem with psychological theories is that one assumes that the categories of crime or deviant behavior can be accepted as given. Douglas (1970:14) has commented:

A crucial element of the traditional absolutist world view dominant in
Western societies has been the taken-for-granted assumption that morals
(right and wrong, morality and immorality, and so on) are not only
necessary and external to man, but also obvious to individuals in any
situation: what is morally right and wrong in any situation has been
assumed to be completely nonproblematic. As a result, moral decision
making has been seen as almost entirely automatic. It was seen as simply
the result of applying the given morals to the given situation. There
was . . . a necessary element of choice; but this choice was thought to be
entirely restricted to the choice between doing right and doing wrong.
There was no choice concerning right or wrong in what ways, or to

what degrees. All of this was given by the iron necessity of God's will, or Being, or nature, or some other absolute.

Until recently, sociologists have almost universally shared this assumption and have taken it for granted in their studies of society in general. This assumption became basic to the whole structural point of view, which many sociologists came to see as the sociological point of view. It led sociologists to concentrate almost entirely on questions concerning the rates of deviance, the exact nature of which they assumed to be obvious, and provided very nicely by official information, and the causes of such deviance, since it seemed very difficult to understand why anyone would do wrong things. Concentration on these problems led to the almost exclusive development of the Durkheimian theory of social rates as the way to study and explain social actions.

In the older, one-sided view of deviance it seemed that the only problematic aspect of the study of deviance was the commission of deviant acts. Straight society was not considered problematic in the least. It was in reaction to this one-sided view of the phenomenon that sociologists with field-work backgrounds began to reformulate their view of deviant behavior and of deviance itself. Whereas Durkheim had said that deviance and crime were necessary in society because the moral boundaries of society were created in the dramatization of the sanctions against evil, the sociologists of the early sixties went one step further and stated that deviance itself was a relativistic conception. In Becker's (1963:9) terms, "social groups create deviance by making the rules whose infraction constitutes deviance, and by applying those rules to particular people and labelling them as outsiders. From this point of view deviance is *not* a quality of the act a person commits, but rather a consequence of the application by others of rules and sanctions to an 'offender.' The deviant is one to whom that label has successfully been applied; deviant behavior is behavior people so label." In this perspective, the deviant labels become problematical, as does the reaction of straight society to behavior that is to be labeled. The absolutist, extrinsic view of the nature of morality is recast in this formulation, and deviance is seen as an interactive process involving negotiation between the straight society (or the agents of that society) and the candidate deviant populations.

The view is revolutionary in the sense that it immediately frees us from the absolutist constraints of past conceptions. The search for the "criminal personality" is ended, because, if the creation of deviance requires collective action on the part of straight society and its candidate outsiders, there is no need to postulate a psychological or psychiatric underpinning for what is clearly a social process. Once again, Becker has stated it succinctly by establishing the term "interactionist" to describe his position (Becker, 1973: 183).

If we can view any kind of human activity as collective, we can view deviance so. What results? One result is the general view I call interactionist. In its simplest form, the theory insists that we look at all the people involved in any episode of alleged deviance. When we do, we discover that those activities involve the overt or tacit cooperation of many people and groups to occur as they do. Donald Roy (1954) discovered that when workers collude to restrict industrial production, they do so with the help of inspectors, maintenance men, and the man in the tool crib. Melville Dalton (1959) showed us that when members of industrial firms steal, they do so with the active cooperation of others above and below them in the firm's hierarchy. Those observations alone cast doubt on theories that seek the origins of deviant acts in individual psychology, for we have to posit a miraculous meeting of individual forms of pathology to account for the complicated forms of collective activity we observe. Because it is hard to cooperate with people whose reality testing equipment is inadequate, people suffering from psychological difficulties don't fit well into criminal conspiracies.

It would seem that the psychiatric or psychological perspective is not as promising as it might intuitively have appeared to be. And what of the social psychological approach? It too suffers from being too "ecological" in perspective. It fails to come to cases in the sense of examining individual deviant careers, noting the contingencies involved, and discussing the points at which straight society affected the career of the deviant. Perhaps we should have been more sensitive to this fact. Hollingshead and Redlich (1958), who carried out the classic studies on social class and mental illness, were aware of it. In the latter part of their work (1958:175–176) they examine the case of two girls who committed similar acts of deviance and who landed up in two different states: one deviant, the other not. The offense was promiscuity; one of the subjects was from the lower class, and the other from the upper class. The upper-class girl was returned to civilian life under the care of a psychiatrist, while the lower-class girl was remanded to a reform school for two years. The upper-class girl was adjudged to have "good prospects" for psychiatric rehabilitation, while the lower-class girl was felt to have poor prospects for psychiatric rehabilitation. Thus, she became a labeled deviant and appeared in the statistics of deviance, whereas the upper-class girl did not. An ecological approach ("ecological" is used here in the sense of "ecological correlation," rather than what anthropologists are accustomed to) would have missed this important difference. Good examples of the interactionists' work can be found in Becker (1963, 1964), Erikson (1966), Friedson (1965), Goffman (1960), Kitsuse (1962), Lemert (1951, 1967), Rubington and Weinberg (1968), Scheff (1966), and Szasz (1961). How does this orientation bear on the studies we criticized earlier? Becker again (1963:9):

Since deviance is, among other things, a consequence of the responses of others to a person's act, students of deviance cannot assume they are dealing with a homogeneous category when they study people who have been labelled deviant. That is, they cannot assume that these people have actually committed a deviant act or broken some rule. Furthermore, they cannot assume that the category of those labelled deviant will contain all those who actually have broken a rule, for many offenders escape apprehension and thus fail to be included in the population of "deviants" they study. Insofar as the category lacks homogeneity and fails to include all the cases that belong in it, one cannot reasonably expect to find common factors of personality or life situation that will account for the supposed deviance.

One example will suffice to show how interaction is involved in the process of being defined a deviant, in this case, a paranoid. It is a good example because we think of paranoia as being psychiatrically defined, rather than an outcome of group interaction. Lemert (1962) reconstructed the process by which a selected group of paranoids arrived at their psychiatric state; he discovered that their condition was the product of a long process of progressive exclusion from a group or groups with which they were affiliated. Typically, a conspiratorial group was formed for the purpose of undermining the candidate paranoid's position in an attempt to remove him from a position of authority in an organization. The conspiracy involved gathering data on his behavior, spying on him, and interacting with him in essentially spurious ways that conveyed little information about his standing in the group. Secret meetings of the group were arranged, or secret communications took place, without his knowledge. The group pooled information about him by way of justifying a more thoroughgoing exclusion, and came to agree among themselves that the candidate's behavior could be labeled as progressively "more dangerous." The candidate paranoid had no way of getting feedback on the consequences of his behavior and was robbed of communication and context by the spurious quality of his relationship with the group. He ultimately believed that people were plotting against him, not because he believed in some delusional "pseudo community" (Cameron, 1943, 1959) but because in fact people *were* conspiring against him. Perhaps the candidate was irritable, closemouthed, and unpleasant to begin with, but it took the reaction of the group to turn him into a paranoid.

But the unconvinced might still say that he "really" is a paranoid, that there is an empirical reality to the state of paranoia. They might say that deviance "really exists out there" in the real world. There is no doubt that the straight world is solving problems by producing deviants by this labeling process, and therefore the categories of deviance have a social reality. But are there "really" murderers, paranoids, and so forth in the world? Are there not well-defined categories to which people who act in certain ways can unambiguously be assigned? And by those criteria can we say that Lemert's subject "really" was a paranoid, and so the social process is a natural one, rather than the self-serving act of a social group?

Since interactionists at times have equivocated a little on this point, it will be useful to state that "really" there are no deviants out there. The deviants have no reality other than the one we accord them by virtue of the social process by which they come to be defined. One important point of this book is to show how the category "witch" is used in the community to label and explain deviant behavior. To the villagers, witches have an objective reality "out there." To me, they do not. I, the sociologist-anthropologist, do not believe that there are people in the world who have the capacity to float foreign objects through the air, insert them into my body, and make me sick or kill me. I do believe that there are people who can make one ill. Even though, like many Western Europeans and Americans, I believe in a most unlikely (Freudian) theory that people close to you are often instrumental in making you sick, I do not believe that there are witches in the world. *We* create the deviants; they are products of our minds and our social processes.

The contemporary view of deviance, then, has two parts, both of which are represented in this study. Good and evil are *both* regarded as problematic, and the explanation of one requires an explanation of the other. The second part of the theory insists that deviance is primarily a sociological phenomenon. That is, social groups create deviance by attention to behavior that they think requires explanation or sanction (or is dangerous or aberrant) and by the collective activity of labeling (i.e., assigning people to the categories of deviance).

When I suggest that the Zapotecs are ahead of us in their view of deviance, I am suggesting two things: first that their views of what is right and what is wrong are inextricably related. I do not think they are entirely conscious of this relationship, but it is perfectly evident in the way they talk and act with respect to what they regard as deviance. Second, they are ahead of us in that they act upon the consequences of the sociological reality of deviant phenomena, or, as I repeatedly say, they *think* sociologically. To anticipate the subject of the book, let me outline the reaction of the Zapotecs to the Hollingshead-Redlich results that people of lower social classes have higher rates of social pathology. To the Zapotec this is readily understandable and not worth explaining. It is not something that requires explanation, because he has a theory about marginal people in which he naturally assumes that people who are distant from one will act in "pathological" ways. (I am assuming that the Hollingshead-Redlich results reflect a middle-class point of view.) In the next chapter I show how the Zapotecs define marginal people in terms of the value system: these are people who are envious by nature, as well as people with whom one must be extremely circumspect ("humble") in one's behavior; they are people whom one suspects of practicing witchcraft. (In the discussion on witchcraft, we will see how witch candidates are drawn from marginal populations.) "Of course marginal people lie about others, and of course they don't believe what they are told. *That's the way such people are.* There is no need to explain such behavior. It is common sense, and no one needs to explain the obvious." Marginal people have no "interests" in others; as the Zapotec would explain, they can expect nothing by way of favors from others, nor others from them. "They are not quite people." If one pushes one's informants for explanations of a psychological nature to account for the malevolence of marginal people, the only answer will be, "it's their nature," which sounds for all the world like, "that's the way it is!" The ill will of marginal people, their strange ways of behaving, and their unwillingness to subscribe to the norms of society do not require explanation, for the explanation resides in the way that society is constituted—in two broad divisions, "inside" and "outside." Outsiders are deviants.

The sociological theme recurs throughout the book. In Chapter Three we will see why the definitions of "abnormal" behavior are sociological and not psychological in nature. I have noticed in talking to Americans about these data that the discussion is quite difficult for them to follow because whenever anyone starts talking about the individual, the inevitable frame of reference that we bring to the conversation is psychological. The Zapotecs think quite differently from us. They don't comprehend the idea of the individual. The basic unit of social analysis for them is not the individual but the dyad, the most elementary *social* unit. Contrast, for example, an American and a Zapotec trying to explain why they regard some person as abnormal. The American will dwell upon inferences about his psychological dispositions and could well summarize his statements by saying something like "he isn't all there," or "he is very neurotic," or "he has a screw loose." Even a word like *together*, which in formal speech refers to social relations par excellence, recently has taken on psychological significance, as in the statement "he's very together." The Zapotec would say, "his kinship relations are defective." He would not mean that he has a bad attitude toward his kinsmen, although that might be true; he means that the person is in an abnormal position because the matrix of relationships in which he is embedded is abnormal. The Zapotecs have a word for *crazy* which is roughly similar to our notion of psychotic, but they don't even regard this condition as deviant. It is not necessary to explain why people are psychotic except to say that they have been struck by lightning, or bewitched, or their souls have been stolen by familiar spirits. It is a condition that does not require explanation, unlike that of having abnormal kinship relations.

This sociological consciousness pervades Zapotec thought. When I examined their hierarchy of deviance (see Appendix One), I found that the most significant way in which it differed from ours hinged upon their predisposition to regard offenses against the social order or conditions that bring about social disorder as being preeminently deviant. Offenses defined by abnormal personality are the least important and are closer to being offenses against manners or etiquette. This is evident in the way they define deviant sexual conduct. There is, however, one form of deviant sexual behavior that they recognize as having importance, adultery. (They are only vaguely aware of homosexuality; they do not distinguish it from hermaphroditism and encounter it only very rarely. The fact that a large number of the people interviewed did not think it deviant at all puts it right at the bottom of the hierarchy of deviance.) Deviant sexual conduct involves the overriding of the boundaries of social categories; adultery is sanctioned, not when one is caught having an extramarital affair, but when one acts so as to confound the major sociological distinction of the society—that is, between insiders and outsiders.

Similarly, in the study of witchcraft we will be able to examine the labeling process and see how the social structure serves to generate witch identifications. The normal social processes that keep the community together—spreading the news and gossip and keeping the informational boundaries coterminous with the community boundaries—produce witches in accordance with the sociological principles of marginality and inside/outside. We see it also in the way they evade the problems of secondary deviance, that is, the changes that take place in a person's conduct when he is labeled a deviant. No labels are accepted; hence, no secondary deviance is created. No one feels that he has to enact a deviant role, because no one accepts the deviant label. "Labeling is necessary for me and for society, but stigmatized scapegoats are not. It does not bother me at all if a bunch of 'outsiders' call me a witch; in any case, they always tell lies, and they are witches for me."

And, finally, we see sociological thinking in the way that members of the community are rehabilitated in cases where judicial authorities outside the community have labeled a villager deviant. The labeled deviants (two convicted murderers) infiltrate the inner group and activate a normal social network, thereby killing the deviant label. When I arrived in the village in 1965, there were two murderers in the community. By 1971 there were none, and the two people in question had not emigrated; they had merely restored their social networks so that they could no longer be defined as murderers. If one cannot have normal relations with a murderer (axiom), and one is having normal relations with X, then X is not a murderer, Q.E.D. And the villagers hotly deny that they are. Rehabilitation is complete.

The intent of this study is to show how in a contemporary traditional community the logic of the interactionist approach to the understanding of deviance has been borne out in detail. Finally, and ultimately, there is no deviance in the world, except as we create it by labeling offenders. Finally, and ultimately, there is no absolute character to the categories of deviance; they are creations of the social order and the ideas that we have about the social order.

2. Values and Social Groups in the Community

The village today has 1,250 inhabitants. It rises in two waves from its base at the municipal building and the church; one travels from below to above, up the wobbling road to the crest of the first wave, and then on to the hill where the most recent houses have been built on the steep hillside. Anyone not used to the appearance of the village will be impressed by the sameness of the adobe houses, which squat cheek by jowl, with flimsy bamboo kitchens leaning against the adobe houses or close by, as though they were huddling together for warmth on a cold day. The main street manages to get over the first rise, but peters out on the downside, clearly unwilling to climb onto the second slope of the village. The view from the top of the first rise is breathtaking—the foothills of the Mixteca Alta.

Beyond the village proper is the river, flanked by the best land. The villagers say that they have no "first-class land." Corn farming is carried out on all classes of land, but the yield on the best wet lands ("second class") near the river is manyfold, greater than on the rocky slopes going up the mountain. Yokes of oxen can be used in the bottom lands by the river, as they can on the gentle slopes beyond the alluvial plain. But the higher slopes toward the mountains cannot be worked with animals; preparing, planting, weeding, and hilling must all be done by hand, with a hoe. This "fourth-class" land is common land; anyone can work it and take the harvest. For many people it represents the only insurance they have against starvation.

Life would be perfect, or so one is led to think, if the rains would only come on time. The rain is the problem. After a season of field work, I felt I would go crazy if anyone ever mentioned the rain again. It is a topic that preoccupies everyone and dominates all conversation from January to July. Some of the happiest faces I have ever seen were those of men standing in a pouring rainstorm one April night when they had taken a gamble, planted their corn early, and won. In most other years they would have lost everything, as they had the year before, and would the next. If it rains, the village prospers. If it does not rain, food gets very scarce, and almost everyone is forced to look for wage work to buy the corn to feed his family. In the bad periods people live on tortillas and salt; all the luxuries are foregone.

The diet, in ordinary times, is simple enough. Tortillas, frijoles, and chile are eaten regularly. On Sunday meat is served with bread and chocolate—it is the feast day. The impoverished diet is only one indication of the easily visible poverty. There are richer people in the community, people who eat well constantly, but there are only five or six of them. Most of the people are so poor as to make one feel like a wastrel or profligate as one watches them count every centavo, guard every grain of corn, and take great pains to concoct meals of grasses and herbs so that they will not have to spend more money on food.

The village is a barnyard—something I noticed the first night I spent there, trying to blot out the bellowings and brayings of the cattle and burros. Flies are everywhere during the day, attracted

by the heaps of manure. Animals and men live together quite happily and symbiotically. Yapping, emaciated, whipped dogs are ubi-
quitous scavengers by day and vicious watchdogs by night.

Although very often first impressions are misleading, there is
one feeling that we share with the villagers. The village is crowded,
and there is no privacy. This becomes clear the very first day when
one goes behind the house to relieve one's self. It is an open place,
and not ideally adapted to what, for us, is a private act. I found
myself grinning self-consciously at passers-by and waving half-
heartedly, trying to be the friendly anthropologist, at the same time
trying to make myself inconspicuous, and fending off the dogs. It
is a very undignified experience. I thought my feeling of claus-
trophobia was just another culturally conditioned response, but
found out later that the villagers feel the same. They like living
together because it gives them a stronger feeling of corporateness
and of support and security, but they realize that it has its incon-
veniences as well. A young married couple explained how frustrat-
ed they were in trying to find a time and a place to have sex without
being accompanied in the act, and how it galled them to have to go
to the fields, as though they were unwed lovers. Jesús brought
home to us the strain of living constantly in the public eye when he
exclaimed that the most beautiful thing about living in our house
in Austin, Texas, was that you could drink, play the record player,
and dance with friends, and *no one, not even the closest neighbors,
knew about it.* The physical and social crowding of the village site
is an important facet of the villagers' lives and is a recurrent theme
in this account. One is forever vacillating between a sense of isolation and a desire for privacy; between a sense of security and a feeling of being watched, vetted, and publicized.

The house lots are not large, and frequently more than one extended family occupies one lot. The houses are small and rarely
used, except for sleeping and performing rituals. All activity goes on
in the kitchen, which is generally a *carrizo* (bamboo) lean-to at the

side of the house, where the women make their tortillas and peer out through the daubed crevices to take in the passing scene. One lives outside. When Jesús was in Texas during the late summer when the heat is formidable, we wanted to sit inside the air-conditioned house, but he found this intolerable and became extremely restless. He preferred working in the unaccustomed heat to being inside a house. This attitude, of course, adds to the problem of privacy in the village. Everything happens outside or behind flimsy walls, and it is very hard to conceal quarrels or fights; a slap can be heard by the neighbors, and it is hard to quarrel in whispers.

In the context of crowded poverty, the villagers have developed a system of values and a social structure that are centuries old. It is that system and that structure that I describe in the rest of the chapter, after a brief introduction into the study of value in general.

VALUES AND DEVIANCE

The major portion of this book is devoted to the discussion of deviance. Here, and in the conclusion, I discuss the question of the general nature of the value system. It is clear that good and evil are interlinked, and that evil is defined in terms of good, and vice versa (see Douglas, 1970: Chapter One); therefore, it is necessary to outline Zapotec conceptions of good in order to understand their notions of evil. But it is not enough to state that good and evil are interlinked. There is a genetic problem involved here, which is usually ignored; that is, we have to account for good or evil. Otherwise, the argument is tautological. In the last chapter of the book, I close the circle and partially escape the tautology by arguing that there is a history and an ecology of good in these communities, and I try to explain where the good came from.

In this chapter I am interested in establishing two things: first, the general dimensions of the value system, and, second, how these dimensions define the most important social categories, the categories of kinship. An axiom of social anthropology is that every institutionalized activity encodes the major value propositions of the society in one form or another. I have chosen to show the interaction of ideas about good and ideas about society in the realm of kinship, because kinship is so important to both the argument and the daily lives of the people I studied.

In the community there are three major ideas that organize the value system. These ideas are the major organizing concepts that discriminate in general fashion between good and evil; namely, "humility," "trust," and "respect." There is one concept that globally refers to bad conduct, and that is "envy." The first three concepts are used constantly by the villagers and assess their own and others' conduct. They serve to summarize what constitute adequate moral strategies for living in the community.

Two questions should be asked in this connection. How do we know that these are the major organizing concepts? How do they tie in with the organization of the domain of deviance? Humility, trust, and respect were important ideas to the villagers because they said so. Over and over again, they would use these ideas to summarize some point of morality or to characterize some general discussion. Obviously, no one said, "The three most important moral ideas are . . ." but the concepts came out so frequently and so forcefully that if the villagers had not had good words to name the ideas, I would have had to make them up in order to account for the data. Equally, they serve to organize the domain of deviance, as I will show in the last part of this chapter. I will reserve the discussion of the implication of this relationship until later and will take up now a description of what the villagers mean when they talk about their value system.

Humility

One of the themes that the villagers emphasize when they describe themselves to outsiders is that they are humble folk. As one of the more eloquent village fathers (self-elected) stated: "This village is different from other villages. Here a man is esteemed for his goodness. Here we can walk the streets, even at night, without a care, because the people are orderly and do not fight. We are humble and poor, and have only our sad village, our wasted lands, and the goodness of God and the saints to help us." Humility is an important expression of the way the villagers would like to believe they want their lives to be. To them, humility is attendance on the desires of others; it is a pervasive sense of equalitarianism. Humility is the absence of selfishness, and it implies a rampant altruism and disregard for one's own immediate welfare, a subversion of self-interest. Humility is obedience to constituted authority. Humility is the granting of the rights of other people to free expression of their opinions and prerogatives. Humility is the ready granting of a favor to others. Humility is the admission that everyone is equal and that everyone is equally poor. Humility is the recognition in one's attitudes and daily conduct of the absence of distinctions between men.

For example, when Augustino, now that he has reached the age of fifty-six, and five of his eight children are married, says, "I am a humble man," he means that he has done his duty to his community, his kinsmen, his *compadres*, his affinals, his children, his co-resident family, and his wife; and in so doing he has not excessively disturbed others. He means that he has worked hard for the sake of hard work and has shown high regard for the spirits of the land and river, as well as for the saints. He means he has no ambition—politically, economically, or morally. He also means that he feels unassailably safe from envy and from witchcraft.

Humility is a style, a way of coping in this demanding life. A typical situation occurs in Augustino's house when someone comes to ask a favor—usually, a small loan. If one has a reputation for humility, as Augustino has, it is known that he will be soft-spoken and kind, and the anxiety that is provoked by the naked vulnerability of the act of petition can be minimized. When the petitioner

arrives, there is an endless round of very soft-spoken small talk in
a specialized high-pitched tone of voice, and all the most formal
Zapotec expressions are used. Often, both people talk at once in
order to put each other at ease, creating a sing-song effect in this
tonal language.

"What are you doing, *compadre*?"
"Nothing. I'm here, that's all; sitting."
"I have come."
"You have come, then."
"I have come to your house."
"You have come to your own house."
"Thank you, *compadre*. I have come for a visit."
"It has not rained, *compadre*."
"No, I went to the fields, *compadre*, and the land wants water very
badly."
"The land is sad, *compadre*."
"It needs water, *compadre*."
"Perhaps it will rain."
"Blessed be the will of God."

The use of high-pitched voice means that this is a formal visit—
a favor is to be asked. After much strophe, antistrophe, and indirect
allusion to the general state of want that prevails in the community,
the favor is hinted, and then drawn up in specifics. The favor will
most likely be denied, because no one could possibly grant all the
favors that are asked of him. It is now that the man of humility
shows his skills. The favor must be denied in such a way as to spare
the petitioner loss of self-respect. The humility of both parties is
emphasized. The equality of all members of the community is
stressed. The poverty and want that afflict all are discussed. All
this is done to assure the petitioner that were it in the power of
the person to grant the favor, there would not be a moment's hesi-
tation, but as the petitioner is in want, and as we are all equal, so
too the petitioner will understand that there is no money, and so

the favor cannot be granted. They state that it is very sad for both of them. Finally, he who came says:

"Well, I came to pay a little visit, and ask a little favor, but I see you cannot."

"This is very sad; I cannot."

"I am going, then."

"You are going?"

"Yes, I am going. Do not say good-bye, because we will be seeing each other again shortly."

"May you go in safety."

Style is very important. If the petitioner feels safe, or if he is in desperate straits and considers someone his last resort, he will suggest that the person is, in fact, wealthier than he claims to be and therefore in a fit position to do the favor. One must put these suggestions aside by stating that appearances are deceiving, and that perhaps the recent misfortunes of sickness, school expenses, and animals dying may have eluded the knowledge of the petitioner. The skill lies in stretching a likely truth into a statement of fact, but not in stretching it so far as to make it unlikely and therefore demeaning to the petitioner. One must be very careful not to leave the slightest hint or suggestion of a lack of trust, because the absence of trust is the harbinger of envy, and envy destroys human relationships and brings with it witchcraft, thievery, and revenge.

Trust

Trust is the second important construct used in interpersonal relations by the Zapotecs. Trust involves character. A good character is one that does not change. A "political man" is the opposite of a trustworthy man, because a political man is all things to all people and changes like a chameleon. Therefore, the ultimate unknowable nature of his heart implies a probability of maleficence. This is in line with the postulate that the Zapotec "think sociologically." Trusting someone means not having to think about erratic or sudden shifts in the way he acts; he can be a constant in the social equation, and therefore can be safely ignored. A trustworthy man is a person who lacks idiosyncrasics that would impinge upon social interaction. Trust involves taking people at their word, taking people at face value (even though "people rarely talk anything but lies and calumny"). Trust involves making no imputation about the soul or psychology of another because "we see the face, but we cannot know what is in the heart." Trust involves not acting upon one's suspicions. Trust involves the truth—one must not lie. Trust is the imputation of reciprocity in relations. It implies the mutual acceptance of obligations and ties that are involved in the initiation of interaction.

The highest insult to a person is to deny the existence of trust. The last desperate attempt to maintain one's self-esteem is to accuse another of perfidy. Social contact between individuals is then precluded, because trust underlies every act of exchange between human beings. Trust means that one can be confident of a person's style; a trustworthy person will be humble and will have respect for another who is momentarily downed. One can drink with a man one trusts, and one cannot drink with any other man. If there is no way to prove trust, one drinks with him. When he suggests that the drinking continue well beyond the casual stage, one keeps on, even though work lapses, errands remain undone, and children and wife ask him to stop.

Augustino had a problem with his friend and *compadre* Joaquin. It was clear that they were no longer on good terms. Joaquin's wife had been spreading vile rumors about Augustino's family and friends and accusing him of ruthless exploitation. Their relationship had become cold and distant. But Augustino's *sagul* (son's father-in-law) had a *cuelga* (name-day ceremony at which much drinking takes place), and Augustino managed to have Joaquin included. They drank together. Next week, Joaquin had a *cuelga* and Augustino went. It was an endurance race between two well-matched men. Four days nonstop the drinking went on, with only brief respites for drunken sleep. At the end of the fourth day, Joaquin said that he would stop drinking and rest the next day. Augustino tottered out of his house, basking in inebriated smiles, saying: "I made it. I stood the course. I did it. I drank as much as he did, and now he wants to go to sleep. I had great respect for his person; I showed that I was a man of trust."

Respect

It is difficult to respect Joaquin, because he is a man of great wealth, probably the wealthiest man in the village. He has land, two yokes of oxen, four milk cows, a huge cart, a big adobe house, a bed, a radio, a store, a son-in-law who is a schoolteacher, sons-in-law who work for him, daughters who live in his house; in fact, he has all that a man could want. He is a man of power and substance and integrity. It is very difficult to show respect to such a man, because respect is based on the subtle manipulation of the symbols of status so as to indicate to the other that you feel he deserves a higher status than he actually has. For another villager to say to Joaquin that "every man is equal; we are all poor humble souls" would be effrontery, because it would suggest that the former was "equal" with Joaquin, and he would resent this. On the other hand, for Joaquin to say that "all men are equal; we are all poor humble souls" is a mark of great respect, because he has brought the other villager up to his level, and thereby obliterated the status difference. True respect is shown to a Zapotec when the social hierarchy of the village is manipulated by others so as to benefit him. The villagers frequently say (particularly when drunk), "I have respect for your person." They mean by this that although one is battered by misfortune in the same stochastic fashion as they are, and although he has failed in much the same way they have, he is still an individual capable of decency and equally capable of harm; and he deserves to be respected.

Respect also implies a fine sense of the prerogatives of others, and in this sense underlies humility. Some men kept on tramping through the forest land when it became known that there was a golden bull, the avatar of the familiar spirits (*chaneques*), living near one of the trails. Not Augustino. He knew that it was not the province of men to disturb the spirit world, and he changed his route. He had respect, unlike another who looked at the golden bull and was blinded by its brilliance.

Were one to ask what the definition of the "good man" was in any of the villages in the valley (and probably throughout traditional Mesoamerica), the reply would be, "He is a person who is willing to do you a favor." The act of asking for, and granting, favors encodes the major value concerns of the villagers. To grant a favor shows that despite momentary relative advantage over the petitioner, one is willing to share substance with him in an altruistic fashion. The villager has responded to the petitioner's admission of humility with humility on his own part. He has shown that despite the clear temptation to indicate a desire to loosen the bond between the two, he chose the way of trust. The petitioner momentarily (and not altogether safely or adventitiously) put the other in a position to show disrespect by indicating that he was willing to accept the differentiation of status that is implied in the petitioner/granter relationship; but he denied the difference and indicated that they were both of the same status by granting the favor. He put the petitioner on a higher level of respectability, but reciprocated by doing the favor, thereby implying that he is a person of such trust that one has no misgivings about his reciprocating. This is a mark of great respect.

Envy

The opposite of humility, trust, and respect is envy. Envy, in its global form, is the explication of what should never characterize human relations. As Wolf (1955) has said of these communities, they are characterized by "institutionalized envy." The rest of this book is devoted to the explication of the notion of envy, and here I characterize it only to sharpen our view of humility, trust, and respect. Envy is a style, a way of coping, just as humility is. The envious man is a person who doesn't know his place in society and is always seeking to find out where and who he is. He is forever making invidious comparisons between himself and others. He is presumptuous and butts into the affairs of others because he doesn't have that fine sense of the subtleties of prerogative that characterize the man of humility and, more especially, of respect. The envious man is too quick to accept the reassurance of others that he is a person of importance. He lacks a well-developed capacity for the control of expression and emotion when he talks with people. He blurts things out. If it is suggested to him that all men are equal in this most democratic and equalitarian of worlds, he, viewing the world in a more pragmatic light, claims that it simply isn't true. "Joaquin," he might suggest, "is very rich." He is overly humble in the sense that he sees riches everywhere, and acts out of an almost paranoid anxiety over his own status. He feels that his neighbor is better off than he. Since his neighbor denies it, and even goes so far as to deny favors on the grounds that he isn't well off, his neighbor is a liar. He does not accept the stylistic conventions that are so important in coping with tension in this crowded, public village. One cannot trust an envious man, because he is self-obsessed, petty, and unruly. One cannot have respect for him, because he is unable to reciprocate. If one were to carry off some brilliant show of respect by indicating in the subtlest of ways that he was truly a much more important person, he would accept it; and instead of insisting on the equalitarian ethic, this person could well go so far as to demean you, which would be inexcusable.

Envy is the dark side of the villagers' character and the dark side of social life. The domain of deviance is a set of variations on the theme of envy. Envy expresses the possibilities of evil in social relations and the fear that the villagers have about the dark side of their character and their own social system. Witchcraft is invariably ascribed to envy; little or no attempt is ever made to examine why envy should apply to a particular case or to speculate on the individual psychological needs of the parties to a witchcraft case that would explain the sharp hostility between them. Why did Hamlet want to kill the king? For vengeance; he did it out of envy. Why did he not kill the king when he was praying? Because he was afraid he would be caught. Why was Hamlet suffering from melancholy? He was sad because his father had died. Everything is ascribed to precipitating events and never to motives or psychology. The unpredictability of the world is caused by events, since character is fixed and unchanging. "We are all the same in the village; all humble, poor men." It is as though the villagers thought that, if one had to account for the actions of one's fellow villagers by a complex analysis of motives and personal idiosyncrasies, one would have to recognize uncertainties and ambiguities that would increase the anxiety of living to an intolerable degree. If one were to admit that the social categories of the village were based on shifting and highly individual, personal factors, then the social world would lose its fixity, and life could not be borne.

Envy, then, is a prime factor. To the villager, envy is an axiomatic primitive, undefined, and undefinable, with enormous explanatory power. It is caused by disjuncture and disharmony between the world as it supposedly is and the seemingly random operations of men in the world. When men contravene the basic assumptions about the way life should be lived, or about the operation of the social world, envy is imputed.

SOCIAL CATEGORIES IN THE COMMUNITY

The general values described above are not just proverbs or pious mouthings of the villagers. The Zapotecs are conscious of them and use the concepts to summarize their feelings about their own moral system. More importantly, they are coded in every institutionalized activity in village life, from corn farming to courting. To understand how they pervade Zapotec social life, one has to understand how the villagers define the categories of kinship— since kinship is the most important idiom of social interaction and since deviance is a product of social interaction.

The villager makes a gross distinction between people who are his kinsmen and those who are not, seeing himself at the center of a set of concentric circles of kinsmen of increasing degrees of distance. As he moves away from himself toward the world of strangers, the general values of humility, trust, respect, and envy take on different configurations. Since deviance and social structure are so closely interrelated in this community, it is important to understand how the language of community organization and the language of morals are inextricably tied together.

Categories of Kin and Nonkin

The community is made up of two kinds of people: "people who live close to me" or what the villager sometimes calls "insiders," and "people who live far away" or "outsiders." "Close to me" is not defined by proximity alone, although it usually includes some neighbors. It is defined by sociological, or kinship, distance. All people "who live close to me" have interests in the villager, and the closer they are, the greater the interest to which they can claim title. (Later, when I discuss deviant sexual behavior, we will see how a villager is constantly concerned with controlling the number and kinds of people who have interests in him and vice versa.) All "people who live close to me" are "something to me," either a kinsman to whom one can demonstrate a relationship, or a neighbor of whom one will readily say, "Yes, he is something to me; he is my neighbor." The rest of the community ("people who live far away") is divided into two categories: "people who are nothing to me," and "people who may be something to me." The latter is a residual category—since people can be transferred from the "nothing" to the "something" category, logically there ought to be a category of "potential somethings"; that is why the villager says that there are people who "*may* be something to me." But that residual category is not defined further (see Fig. 1); it is a terminal taxon.

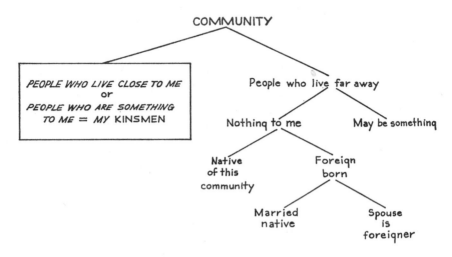

Fig. 1. Taxonomy of the Major Social Categories of the Community

People who are "something to me" are kinsmen. They may be genealogically defined kinsmen to whom one can demonstrate a relation. They may be people to whom one is close and whom one has assimilated into one's kinship set in one of three ways: he may have given them a fictitious title, calling them "uncle," or "brother," or "grandfather," even though he is perfectly aware that they are not recognized kin; he may have entered into a ritual relationship with them by being the sponsor of a family religious event; or he may have extended a tie that had remained cool for years, or perhaps for generations, and assimilated the person into the "affinal," "fictive," or "cousin" category. It is very hard not to be a cousin to another villager. The community has been settled for centuries and is endogamous; therefore, if one wishes, one can activate a remote tie of cousinhood with almost everyone. More commonly, one can extend the meaning of one of the two most emotionally important kinship categories—*sagul* (in-law) or *mbal* (*compadre*). Any relative by marriage is eligible for the *sagul* category (relations up to five links away have been recorded), and any agnatically (patrilineally) related kinsman of the original sponsor and beneficiary of baptism, marriage, or confirmation can call himself *mbal*. This is not a routine act or the conferral of a courtesy title, as is the creation of fictitious kinsmen or assignment to "cousin." *Mbal* and *sagul* are the two most important relationships of respect outside the nuclear family and one's own line; making someone a *sagul* or *mbal* is not an act lightly undertaken.

Kinsmen

The concentricity of the kinship system shows up very clearly in the villagers' perception of the relative position of the categories of kinsmen. The terminological system is very much like our own. A componential analysis for aficionados of kinship is presented in Appendix Two. For the purposes of understanding the sociology of deviance, it is important to see how the ideas of good and evil are encoded in and define the kinship categories. The taxonomy, for example, indicates a most important feature of the categorical system: there is a large gap between "people who live close to me" and "people who live far away." People who live far away are the marginal people described in the first chapter. They are people who are predisposed to envy, to lie, and to act in erratic and malicious ways. They are people of the outside who are most likely to be witches, and if a villager has to find a witch, he will look for one among them. He does not even recognize genealogical kinsmen who are members of the outside; the act of recognition is the way in which he brings them across the taxonomic divide into the inside. People of the outside have no interests in him, nor he in them. He cannot expect favors of them, nor they of him; they have nothing to exchange. "People who live far away" are people whom one will not trust and from whom one cannot expect a great deal of respect. One must be exceedingly humble with such people, because not to be so would invite their envy, and "people who live far away" are predisposed to envy one by nature. Thus, the act of recognizing a previously unrecognized kinsman involves decisions to change one's relations with him. As a result, the taxonomic distinction divides the community into two gross categories—the insiders and the outsiders. This categorical distinction will be seen impinging on the world of deviance in the analysis that follows.

The overall distinction between insiders and outsiders encodes the major ideas of the value system, as well as the concentric ordering of the categories of kinship. There are trust and respect for all members of the category of "people who live close to me." But the distance from ego in Figure 2 is not arbitrary, because it varies inversely with trust and respect, and directly with humility. The greater the distance between a person and someone else, the greater the probability that envy will be mobilized by one against the other. Since humility is the style that copes with envy, they both increase with distance (see Fig. 3).

Of the four major value concepts, "trust" and "envy" are the easiest to map onto the kinship model. The potential for trust decreases and the potential for envy increases as one moves away from ego. There is a quantum leap as one crosses the border from "people who live close to me" to "those who live far away." "Respect" is more complicated because there are other influences that affect it, among them, relative age. For example, if the person is a young unmarried woman, she will show a great deal of respect to her courtesy kinsmen because they will be older, and some of them males. She will not respect her parents, in the sense we have been

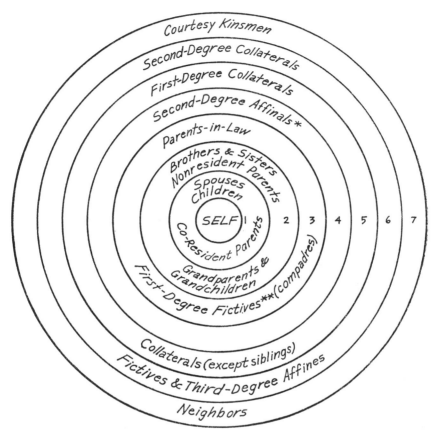

Fig. 2. The Conscious Model of Kinship

* See Appendix 2. Second-degree affinals are parents-in-law and siblings-in-law. Third-degree affines are those related by marriage, but more distantly removed than either the spouse or second-degree affinals.

** First-degree fictives are those who were linked by the act of sponsorship, i.e., the actual *tatmbal, shinbal,* and *mbal*'s (or, in Spanish, *padrino, ahijado, compadre*).

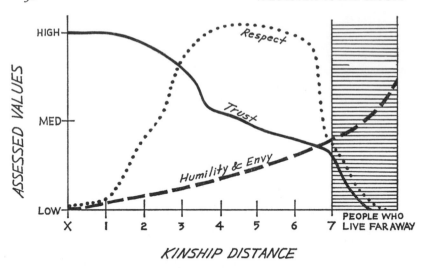

Fig. 3. Kinship Distance and Values

using the word here. Her fictive kin will often be her companions, and she will give them an increment of respect, but very little compared to the respect she will pay her godfather, who sponsored her baptism. As one gets older and becomes more prestigious, one removes one's self from the familiarity of younger ways and becomes more of a person of respect as well. In neither case does one respect people "who live far away." In that sense respect and trust are similar. One does not know "people who live far away," but more importantly, one does not have sufficient contact with them to develop the understanding that is the basis for a show of respect. Neither does one respect the innermost circle of kinsmen—a person would not be expected to manipulate the symbols of status so as to reflect flatteringly on either his wife, his children, or his parents. He obviously trusts them. He does respect his affinals and his *compadres*.

"Humility" is also complex. One is not humble with his inner kinsmen but is very humble with those "who live far away." Augustino could feel unassailably safe from witchcraft and envy because he knew well that there were very few people in the community who could "outhumble" him, and so he could either disarm, or at the least not evoke, the potential envy that always exists across the taxonomic divide. Highly patterned relationships do not require a good deal of humility. A Zapotec does not have to be humble to his father-in-law or his godfather, because he is so intent on respecting him that their relationship is well defined and does not require the lubricant of a demonstration that one knows how to do favors, and act properly. It is almost impossible for a villager not to act properly with those categories of kinsmen.

Conclusion: Values, Kinship, and Deviance

People who have never had occasion to live in a traditional community or have never done field anthropology may wonder why anthropologists pay so much attention to the business of kinship. There are many reasons, but the most compelling, in my opinion, is that kinship provides people of traditional communities with a vocabulary of discourse, an explanatory paradigm, and a set of reference points for their thinking, not only on the sociological plane, but also on the level of cosmology, ritual, and economic and political activity. The amount of "kinshipping" that one has to do in daily intercourse is truly staggering. Every time one walks down the street one encounters kinsmen of every kind, and one moves through a variety of role relationships even while on the most casual errand. In a Mesoamerican community the anthropologist becomes enmeshed in kinship relations by making *compadres*. I well remember doing errands with a *compadre* of mine, being taught my extended relations, and thinking how exhausting the whole business was. One is hemmed in (and supported) on every side by kinsmen, who are the major social reality of everyday experience. Ritual in these Zapotec communities is an explication of the kinship paradigm in that it arranges people in kinship groups and symbolizes the distinctions between them.[1] Economic cooperation, which is necessary for survival, requires a reliance upon one's kinsmen for help in the fields, or in roofing a house, or for lending money when some disaster like a wedding or the death of an animal occurs. Political activity means the marshaling of support for activities through kinsmen, and the person who wins political battles is usually the person who can activate the kinship network most effectively. It is not surprising that thinking in terms of kinship is a most natural and almost inevitable act.

As has been shown, the major value concepts of the community define the categories of kinship and provide axes for their relations. To talk about kinship is to talk about values, the global values of the community. This is perhaps true of all societies. Schneider (1968) has shown that in American kinship the contrasts between "blood" and "contractual" relations are worked out in the definition of kinship categories and that this opposition is subsumed by a higher-order opposition between "nature" and "law," which is central to American thought. He finds that to understand what concepts Americans use when they think about kinship, one has to understand their master distinction between "home" and "work," between "cognatic" and "erotic" love, and that "sexual intercourse" is a master symbol of American kinship, relations, and culture.

In Zapotec it is clear that kinship equals values (in the sense that I have discussed it above), and that values equal deviance, for without good there is no evil, and each serves to define the other. Douglas (1970:4) has a good discussion of the necessary opposition between good and evil, when he says:

In our everyday lives morality and immorality, respectability and disreputability, and other worldly, and the this-worldly, the sacred

---

[1] El Guindi (1971, 1972) has an extended discussion of the relationship between the categories of kinship and ritual in Zapotec communities.

and the secular—each term necessarily implies the existence of its opposite and, consequently, depends on its opposite for its own meaning and, above all, for much of the force that it exerts on our own lives . . .

The most general consequence of this necessary linkage in social meaning between good and evil is that we will always have evil at the same time that—and precisely because—we have good. Going further, we should expect that the more intense the belief in good, or the striving for it, the more intense will be the belief in evil, or the attacks on good. An age of saints, then, will also necessarily be an age of satans or demons and vice versa. An individual striving for goodness will to the same degree be striving against evil and vice versa . . .

And, at the same time that good necessarily implies the opposite of evil (and vice versa) good necessarily implies a categorical contrast; if there is a good type, there must be an evil type.

Good implies evil, good implies kinship, kinship implies evil—the circle is complete. Being deviant is being unable to be a good kinsman. Deviance is a situation that is characterized and defined by deteriorated or abnormal kinship relations. Kinship in its general sense as a coherent body of ideas is a powerful moral philosophy.

And this is why the Zapotec is not making some breathtaking intellectual leap when he rejects psychological explanations for deviance in favor of sociological ones; it is simply common sense to him and arises naturally and logically out of the way that he defines and categorizes his social world.

3. Deviance and the Social Structure

The lexicon of deviance does three things: it defines what is evil, it stigmatizes the conduct and the people who engage in evil, and it serves to warn of the pitfalls and punishments that attend evil. In a word, it guards and guarantees the conditions of ordered existence and represents a coherent system of ideas about the nature of society, of order, and of the world. Every society picks and chooses its own particular specialities of sin, and societies are characterized as much by what they ignore, or fail to define, as by what they pick out for definition. In modern urbanized societies, where prevailing ideas and conventional wisdom change rapidly, the major problem is often one of handling and adjudicating between novel varieties of sin that different groups or sectors activate, define, and promulgate for the acceptance of their definition of the right kind of ordered existence. The battle takes place in the political, communicational, and judicial arenas, and those whose definitions are accepted are usually (but not always) those who either gain or retain their political offices as well as the power to declare what is moral and proper. In stable, small-scale societies the battle is not of this kind. The ideology is fairly secure, and the battles take place over who shall be stigmatized or labeled. In stable societies novel forms of deviance are rare, and there is a much wider latitude of agreement over what constitutes evil. Moral development is much more surely signposted by the lexicon of deviance in traditional societies than in modern, urban societies because there is a greater assurance that the rules will not be changed from day to day. Therefore, if one looks at what is defined as evil and what is not defined as evil, one can gain comparatively greater insight into the general ideas of morality in traditional society than in urban society. Homosexuality is the example of undefined conduct in Zapotec. It is a common-sense category of deviance to us, and if the Zapotecs were given to homosexuality, doubtless there would be a great deal of moral ideology that commented on the practice. But they are not. The division between men and women is so clear, so absolute, so well marked, and so unquestioned that the mere thought of engaging in homosexual behavior is foreign to them. Sexual activity is only defined for intersex relations.

It is the same for severe mental illness or psychosis. I realized after I had collected the main body of materials on deviance that I had no material on mental illness. When I discovered this lacuna, I hoped that it was because of the very pedestrian (ethnosemantic) way in which I had collected my data. Good ethnosemantic methodology requires that questions of informants be culturally relevant, preferably elicited from the informant himself. The Zapotecs had made up no questions about mental illness, although we had been talking about deviance for months. So I gathered more data and found out that there were people who were "crazy," but that the condition was very simply defined. One could not be sure, but it had something to do with the soul and was symptomized by agitated motor behavior, ataraxia, violent purposeless movement, and the inability to talk in ways that people could readily understand. Crazy people ate, drank, and socialized with everyone else, and

most of the time their behavior was unremarkable. One man regularly went into psychotic states and equally regularly emerged from
them, but the villagers were not that interested in his condition.
Another man sometimes had to be restrained within the house, if
barring the door of a bamboo hut can be called restraint. Crazy
people were not stigmatized in any way, even though it was judged
unlikely that they would be elected to a powerful political office;
but in any case, they would not seek office. If they had delusional
symptoms, no one was particularly interested in them or felt that
they had special powers of any kind. The etiology of the cases was
generally similar: each person had experienced an encounter with
a supernatural agent that had somehow robbed him of his soul,
whether the agent was a particularly malicious familiar spirit,
Changing Woman, or the spirit of the lightning. The level of
definition was very low, and, practically speaking, there were no
culturally defined psychotics in the community (although there
were certainly people we would define as psychotic).

There was a condition that the villagers recognized as carrying
moral stigma, however, and regarded in much the same way as we
regard mental illness; this I have called "abnormality." The Zapotecs have many words for it and a good deal of ideology. Like
all the major forms of deviance, it is defined sociologically, and
not psychologically (I discuss it in the next section). In fact, I
propose that all the major forms of deviance are defined sociologically and that the lexicon of deviance protects the vitals of the
social organism (and not the person) by stigmatizing sets of relations that would be incongruent with the Zapotec ideas of a properly
constituted social order. The example of "abnormality" is used
to discuss the definition of deviant behavior. A look at examples of
deviant behavior that rank very high in the Zapotec estimates of
evil (the deviance items are given in Appendix One, along with
their rankings) shows that they all involve behavior that can readily
be interpreted as having injurious repercussion to the network of

relations of the inside. Conflict is discussed below as a sin of commission against the insiders' network, but I also discuss sins of omission which have the same effect, and note in passing that the lexicon of deviance here, as elsewhere, is differently defined for men and for women. Finally, I talk about the conditions that give rise to social order; in particular, the conditions that permit reciprocal exchange and explain some apparent anomalies in the Zapotec conceptions of deviance.

ABNORMALITY

The Zapotecs feel that people who do not have a proper set of relationships with people of the inside are abnormal and somewhat less than fully human, much in the way that we regard people who are mentally ill. There is one man in the community, Alejandro, who represents a visible, developed case of "abnormality." Of course, he is not the only person felt to be abnormal; everybody has his own list of candidates for the label. But Alejandro is a good example of abnormality. Eusebia talks about him.

He doesn't allow kids to go into his patio. In fact, he comes all the way over here to take a shit. He used to fight with his children a great deal. He used to tell his oldest boy that he didn't belong to them, but rather was a bastard by some lover of his mother. He had another kid, a boy, who moved away when he got married because he couldn't stick it out with his father. Alejandro really has an ugly way about him. Sometimes his children would go to work with him in the fields, and if they didn't know how to do something, then Alejandro would grab a stick and scream, "You stupid fucking animal . . . !" and would beat them as if they were burros, shouting at them, "Go home to your goddamn mother!"

He would go home, and dinner wouldn't be ready and he would say: "You lazy fucking woman, what have you been doing? Why isn't my dinner ready?" Then he'd grab something and beat her like an animal.

The two major components of abnormality appear quite clearly in Eusebia's brief characterization of Alejandro, although at first they may not be completely obvious. Alejandro is abnormal because he defines his personal space in such a way as to contravene the categorical imperative—were everyone to define what is his alone the way that Alejandro does, there would be no community. He is abnormal also because he acts in such a way as to render impossible adequate social relations within the inner group of kinsmen, or "insiders." He is disturbed by children. Everyone becomes upset by children's naughtiness from time to time, but Alejandro performs a very antisocial act: he excludes them from what he defines as his space. Children in small, traditional communities serve important purposes, as Hotchkiss (1968) has pointed out. They are information gatherers and transporters. They are the intelligence operatives of the community. Because they are defined as nonpersons, they can penetrate into scenes where persons, and particularly alien persons, would not be able to penetrate. Since one has to take a great deal of care in interpersonal relations in the community and control a great deal of information in order to "respect" people in the proper fashion, one has to know what the current state of affairs is, that is, who is fighting with whom, whether gossip is true, who is doing favors for whom, what the current economic status of people close to one is, and so on. Children gather this information. But, if adults define their social space as Alejandro does, penetration is difficult. One will not have the necessary information and will become isolated from the rest of the community. If everyone defended the margins of his social space the way Alejandro does, there would be no community.

In addition, Alejandro not only maintains impermeable boundaries to his social space, but also defines that space unconventionally, which is what Eusebia means when she wonders about his defecation routine. Eusebia does not live that close to Alejandro, and he is going to some considerable trouble in not defecating in his own living place. It is not that Alejandro is peculiar in thinking that human feces are dirty or undesirable; everyone feels that way to some extent. It just does not occur to any normal Zapotec that human beings cannot coexist with their own excrement. It would be difficult to feel this way because they live in a barnyard. Manure is everywhere in the village. Animals live on one's patio, in one's house, and near it. People and animals share the same living space, and there is nothing unnatural about this ecumenism; the symbiosis between man and his animals is recognized and important. In fact, the more usual way of saying that a person is abnormal is to say outright that "he won't let animals into his patio," or that "he throws rocks at any stray that wanders near his house." And the villagers do not worry about the possible damage that might occur to animals from someone throwing rocks at them—it is the way they normally herd animals. People who don't allow animals on their patio are being more than fastidious; they are declaring an antagonism to an important relationship that all men have with other beings sharing their house. (It should be pointed out that the house in Zapotec is *the* central symbol of the ritual context, and rituals, in turn, act to define and affirm the primary distinctions of the social order.)[1] Alejandro defines his social space in a very peculiar fashion, and, by tampering with the important relationship between man and animal, he is tampering with a central symbolic and economic relationship.

Abnormal people have defective relationships with the inside as well, with their children, their wives, or their affines (relatives by marriage). Alejandro denies that he is his children's father. He is willing to wear horns so that he can vent his ill feelings upon his children. He picks fights with his children, despite the fact that the prototypical relationship of amity is between a man and his sons. A normal man would do none of these things. Were any normal

---

[1] Once again I am referring to the work of El Guindi (1971, 1972).

man so outraged by the conduct of his son as to warrant an intense emotional outburst, he would formally curse the child, drive him out of the house, and order him to find a living by "begging torti-llas in the houses of strangers." Since Alejandro does not do so, he is enmeshed in a bizarre set of relationships with his own children.

The theme of a defective relationship with one's wife recurs in the discussions of abnormality. For example, the abnormal person appears to be very insecure about his sexuality and authority. While this might seem natural to us, with our Freudian notions that relate sexual with executive competence, the Zapotecs are not Freudian at all. They feel that men perform sexually just as naturally and normally as they breathe and eat. Impotence is always attributed to external factors, either illness or witchcraft. In any case, it is not a condition that has moral status and psychological correlates.

Santos once explained that wives of abnormal people had a par-ticularly difficult time, because their husbands would use sexual threats and abandonment to assure their authority in the household. "This type really likes the women, and likes to give his wife hell as well. He needles her about his authority in the household, and she gets frightened because she knows she can't stand up to the sexual attractions of the younger girls." But perhaps more indicative of the kind of neurotic attitude about sexuality that underscores this incomprehensible insecurity about sexual competence is the way such people openly molest women. An abnormal person may pub-licly attempt to fondle the breasts of a young girl; and he won't be drunk either, which would make it understandable. Santos again: "He'll go out into the street with anyone, and make a great row, and if there are not men to drink with him, he'll find any old woman that he meets and make a pass at her publicly." There are ample opportunities for culturally permitted sexual liaisons in this community. It is abnormal to make so much out of the facts of bio-logical endowment and sexual competence, which accrue to every-one by natural right.

It is not just the tie between parent and child or between man and wife that is defective in an abnormal relationship. Conduct that abuses the tie between affinals is even more predictive of such a person. Consider, for example, the mother-in-law (a neighbor of Amelia's, though not a person who "lives close to her") who has reduced her son-in-law to a blubbering, quavering nonentity. She has exaggerated to an unthinkable degree the authority that naturally accrues to her. She enters disputes that are none of her business and she punishes her son-in-law in ways that contravene moral and symbolic limits of the relationship. Amelia clearly regards her as abnormal:

If this lady doesn't like something that her son-in-law is doing, she will grab and beat him, and beat her daughter too. Her son-in-law weeps because she mistreats him so badly. She is quite rich and sends corn to her daughter [i.e., inverts the exchange relationship; they should be sending corn to her] and tells the son-in-law to go to the mountain to fetch wood, and if he doesn't go, she beats him. Worse, if the son-in-law beats her daughter [which he is entitled to do for bad role performance or reasonable suspicion of a special kind of adultery], she'll round on him and beat him too.

These sociological propositions define abnormality in this community. It goes without saying that the abnormal person does not engage in the proper forms of ritual conduct. In fact, Alejandro went to a saint's day party some years back and was turned away because he hadn't gone through the prescribed ritual greetings and offerings with his *compadres*. It is unthinkable to turn someone away from a party. When people announce their parties they are usually frightfully anxious that no one will come, or if they do come, that they won't get ritually drunk. Everyone of the inside is most welcome. Alejandro does not need a psychiatrist; if anything, he needs a consulting sociologist who will straighten out his table of organization, and therein lies the difference between his society and ours in the way that abnormality is defined.

THE INSIDERS: SINS OF COMMISSION, SINS OF OMISSION

The most serious forms of deviance are concerned with relationships of the inside. Sins of commission are most heavily sanctioned, but sins of omission are high on the list and are also regarded as serious. The Zapotec might wistfully agree that good fences make good neighbors, but he would add that good fences make bad communities or, at least, bad Zapotec communities, and it is not surprising that fighting with one's neighbors is considered a serious form of deviance by the villagers.

Fortunately, Bi'či (her real nickname in Zapotec means "unkempt") and Santos are not close kinsmen. If they were, the intolerable situation that exists between them would have to have been settled long ago by their respective godfathers. They have had a quarrel for as long as I have known them. They are neighbors. They are not too dissimilar in personality, although Bi'či has more grit than Santos. She is very outspoken and quick-witted, while Santos fancies himself as a person with a fair degree of style, even though he will occasionally do some very foolish things (he recently went running around the village, roaring drunk, tearing his clothes off). Bi'či is always needling Santos, and Santos is always attempting to stop her by matching her wit with male dignity. He has little success in this. Bi'či accuses Santos of being "abnormal" because he sent his wife to rail at her for allowing her child to pick a fight with Santos's "well-behaved" children. Santos wants an ordered life, but he lives next door to a woman (Bi'či) whose household must be the most disorderly in the valley. Animals, fleas, dirt, noise, and children are constantly spilling out of her house into Santos's life, and he cannot bear it. As soon as Bi'či's husband was beginning to get ahead by making wooden beams for sale, Santos accused him of stealing the beams. The husband retaliated by accusing Santos of embezzling money from the treasury of the Comisariado, since Santos was secretary of that organization. It galled Santos that

he could not extrude Bi'či from his world, as he was constantly trying to do. It galled Bi'či that a person like Santos could even *become* secretary of the Comisariado. "Christ, that idiot can't even
write his name!" she once told me. They are often cited by the villagers as a case of the kind of deviant conflict that, if widespread,
would lead to community break-up. It would be quite intolerable if
all people carried on this way, and both Bi'či and Santos have been
warned by the authorities and by their kinsmen about their behavior. But they persist and probably will for the rest of their lives.
Since conflict of this kind is contagious and hard to contain, it is
not surprising that it is controlled by stigmatization, for it is a very
serious form of deviant behavior.

Less obvious (and less sinful, though still seriously so) is behavior that indicates a withdrawal from the inner group. Stigmatized
forms of behavior are of two kinds: general behavior that applies
equally to all people and behavioral forms that are sex specific. Any
behavior that permits the inference that one is treating an insider
like an outsider is severely sanctioned. If one is verbally aggressive
to someone, or if one lies to someone or refuses to believe someone,
one is treating him as a stranger, or as people who live far away.

Being verbally aggressive is a sign that one is not going to com-
mit oneself to the usages that define and permit interpersonal
exchange. Recall the conversation between Augustino and the
would-be borrower of money: Augustino lied when he stated (or
suggested) that perhaps the would-be borrower was unaware of the
stringent financial situation that Augustino was in because of the
illness of his wife, the premature death of the animal, and the
school expenses. He wasn't in any more of a stringent financial situation than usual, and none of those things had quite taken place
in the time framework that he was suggesting. The appropriate response for the would-be borrower is to display surprise and sym-
pathy, all the while hinting that things are tough for everyone in
this community, and that perhaps the lender has a little more cash

than he is suggesting he has. This roundelay, this laborious circum-
locution, the periphrasis, is an important part of the indication of
"humility." There are people, however, who want to withdraw, to
avoid their responsibilities to people close to them. They cut
through these conventions and are likely to say, "Your wife hasn't
been sick a day for ten years," which would be extremely rude, or
they would turn prosecutor, and ask, "When was your wife sick?
Why was she sick? How much did it cost?" This would be more
than a solecism; it would indicate that such a person was not a
party to the conventions of civilized conversation. It would be tantamount to stating that he was not sufficiently in command of himself to enter into civilized exchange and therefore no longer to be
considered part of the inside group of "people who live close to
me."

Lying to people in one's inner group is a clear sign that one is
escaping. To lie is to define oneself as a "person who lives far
away." Eusebia was very clear on this, even though she turned the
argument around. "Sometimes we sell a young cow for [Mex.]$1,-
500 or $2,000," she said one day with a resigned sigh, "but the
people who live far away don't believe it is 'good money.' They say
it is money from the devil, and it's a lie. That's the way those people
are. They lie!" Santos tells the story of his Uncle Julio, who got involved with Maximino in a way that made them close companions
and defined their relationship as one between "people who live
close together." Julio, for reasons I don't know, didn't want this
kind of a relationship with Maximino, despite the fact that he had
initiated it himself; he resorted to a simple stratagem to terminate
and redefine the relationship—he lied. "Uncle Julio lost his money
and said that Maximino had taken it out of his pocket book. He
had had eighty pesos and had been drinking with Maximino. But it
wasn't true, because the money had fallen out of his pocket, and
Maximino's little girl had found it. It was lying on the ground in
the place where Julio had gone to urinate. Uncle pressed charges

and Maximino was hauled before the authorities, who immediately dismissed the case when they found out what had happened."

Another way of indicating the same message is to "be unbelieving." If a villager refuses to believe someone, it is not just that he is implicitly accusing him of being a liar (which would declare the relationship to be between outsiders), but he is also refusing to defend jointly their social identity as members of the same community. This becomes clear in the example of an act of thievery that happened in the local market town. "One of the people who won't believe anything was in town when one of the village women had her wallet taken by a stranger. The woman rushed up to him and asked if he had seen the person who took it, and he said he hadn't because he didn't want to believe that the woman's wallet had been stolen." This is exactly how he would have behaved if a person from the neighboring village had asked him whether he had seen the wallet stealer. But when a person of his own group (and the implication is that the woman has "insider" credentials) confronts him, he retreats by being an unbeliever.

Women are more oppressed by the value system than are men. This is probably true in many societies, although anthropologists have not been wont to pursue the point in their studies. Certainly it is true in Zapotec, and I am not referring to that cloistering of women that is found throughout Latin America. In a Zapotec village women are expected to carry the moral system to a greater degree than men. They assume the moral burden of maintaining the relationships of the inside. They must be deferent to men, they must take responsibility for the children, and, perhaps most of all, they have the responsibility for the day-to-day maintenance of the house and all the members in it, even though they must retire unto themselves when the house comes alive and turns into a place of ritual. As in many communities, their work is denigrated, not directly, but indirectly. It is not defined as activity that requires mythical, ritual, or ideological definition and development. Things that are interesting by cultural definition here, as elsewhere, are done by men. Women's work is unmarked, routine, unremarkable, and not culturally elaborated (cf. Garretson Selby, 1972). There are no rituals for the making of tortillas; there are for planting the corn. Women make the tortillas and men plant the corn. Perhaps more important is the fact that the work and the attention that women have to devote to the inside group are constant. A man may be lazy for a day, and the corn will not wither, but, if a woman is lazy for a day, no one will eat. It is not surprising that the value system (and the lexicon of deviance) bears harder upon the woman than the man, for her work is more crucial, unrecognized, and less rewarded.

Nor is it surprising that the cultural expectation exists that women will show greater acceptance of and commitment to the value system than will men. The villagers recognize this, as do most observers. O'Nell and I tried to indicate in our study of the incidence of "fright sickness" (O'Nell and Selby, 1968), or *susto*, that the disease was in part a characteristic of the woman's role. Women are more constrained by highly defined role demands than are men, and as a result they use the pretext of an illness—*susto*—to withdraw from the group of close insiders. Typically, a woman who becomes *asustada* gets a "generalized symptom" of illness—fever, loss of appetite, sweating, headache—as well as the defining symptom: an unwillingness to communicate. Sometimes this unwillingness to communicate resembles catatonia. Women have been known not to say a word for days on end. They sit on a small sleeping mat to the side of the fire without moving. They are frightened by sudden noise or movement. The cure is composed partly of some incantations, partly of some egg potions, but mainly of a good deal of tenderness, love, and care. *Asustadas* are relieved of their duties and their responsibilities. Nothing is expected of them. They are left alone to rest and recuperate. The condition can last for months.

Susto can be called "good," or "acceptable," withdrawal in the sense that it leaves the relationships within the inner group intact.

Being outspoken, lying, and being an unbeliever are "bad" forms of withdrawal for both women and men. Fighting and child abandonment are two forms of withdrawal that are defined as deviant things that women do to withdraw. The distinctions here are difficult. We must distinguish between fighting (in general) and battles with one's neighbors, which is what Bi'či and Santos do. They are quite distinct in community thinking, and in Zapotec. Both men and women battle with their neighbors, and thus act in a deviant fashion. When men fight (in general) it is not a deviant activity, because "that's what men do." When women fight it is a deviant activity. An explanatory device can be borrowed from the Zapotec, using their words *ši'an* (strong anger) and *ti'up* (fright), the latter being the predisposing condition for fright sickness (*susto*). Men get *ši'an*, or strong emotional outbursts, and they fight, and that's the way they are. There is nothing either deviant or remarkable in that. *Ši'an* and fighting are a part of the man's role. Men do not get *susto*; they do not suffer *ti'up*. Women and children do. If a man becomes *asustado*, he is acting as a deviant because he is retiring in an unacceptable way from the demands of the inside group. Similarly, for a woman *susto* is acceptable; *ši'an* is not. Women do not have strong emotional outbursts. Thus, when a community member says that "fighting" has taken place, he means it has taken place between women, or that a woman is involved.

It is the same with child abandonment. Men abandon their children just as women do, but when the community members say that a man has abandoned his children they mean that he is on the prowl sexually. It is exciting and something all the men would like to do, and if it leaves the woman stranded temporarily, "that's the way men are." Men abandon their children a lot; that is, they leave their wives and take up residence with other women. In the summer of 1968 five men were living with women who were not their wives. When women abandon their children, however, it is a deviant act of withdrawal, an escape from the system, and therefore in-

tolerable. Women do, in fact, abandon their children; they tire of
them. They talk about a profound urge to get away from them,
about a kind of apathy that creeps over them so that they "go and
buy their tortillas" instead of staying at home and making them by
hand. They don't want to perform those essential household tasks
that are necessary for the inner group. All women have the urge to
abandon their children from time to time, but most resist. The
most serious form of the urge expresses itself in a revulsion at the
sight of one's baby. Women sometimes get sick to their stomachs
just looking at their babies and abandon them in the sense that they
fail to look after them. Using a technical expression, they say, "I
cannot bear to look upon the face of my baby," and they recognize
this to be an illness associated with nausea, dizziness, and vertigo.
The affliction is a recognized and comprehendible syndrome, even
though it is very dangerous, and in more than several cases has
been fatal to the child. Every year at least one child dies of "neglect" arising from abandonment, and, despite the striking importance of the woman's commitment to her children as a token of
her commitment to the norms of the inner circle, it does occur. Unlike *susto*, which is neither deviant nor immoral, abandonment is
immoral. It is a supreme act of withdrawal on the part of the
woman from the core relationships of the network.

I was unaware for a long time of the way in which escaping the
system was censured. One of the incidents that enlightened me as
to the nature of the demands being put upon the community members was a family quarrel that I, adventitiously, happened to attend. This story displays human reactions to the value system and
gives one of those rare insights into people's strivings to cope with
their own morals and the difficulties and tensions that are involved.

The fight, like most family fights, was not about the declared
subject. The principals, Bi'či and her aunt, were sitting in their
house husking corn. Bi'či's husband was outside working on some
tie rods for the ox cart. There was obvious tension in the air. Bi'či

and her aunt had not been getting along well, and there had been skirmishes over the children. The aunt felt the children weren't as well behaved as they ought to be, and Bi'či felt that her aunt should mind her own business even though she couldn't say so because her aunt was a kinsman, older, and therefore deserving of trust. There was sporadic conversation that afternoon, and the aunt happened to remark in what to me sounded like an innocent, conciliatory voice, "Isn't it nice how we can all be here in one house, just the family with the children and all." There was silence, and then one of the most violent emotional explosions I have ever seen, certainly the most violent for these quiescent villagers. Bi'či started to scream at her aunt; she threatened her, she terrified the children, she started to cry, then stopped and leveled one of the most venomous tirades at her aunt that I have ever heard, concluding with a statement close to the following: "You may have gotten me a husband, and you may have built me this house and given me some land, but I am not going to feel bad about it. I am okay now, and you haven't got a goddamn thing, you one-eyed hag, you ugly old bitch. You wander around like a whoring prostitute, and you never have to worry about getting knocked up by a man because you can't have any children . . . you killed your children and ate them, just like the bitch you are. You are mad at me because I *do* have children. I am a *real* woman, and you are old and wrinkled and abandoned."

At first I thought Bi'či had gone momentarily crazy. Like a proper villager I condemned her conduct and was embarrassed for the aunt, feeling humiliated for and with her. It wasn't until I got to know Bi'či quite well that I recognized what she was saying in this most remarkable speech. It was a plea to be left alone. It was a plea to be let off the hook. She was begging to be allowed to go her own way without being constantly judged, constantly grateful, and perpetually deferent. Bi'či is a very intelligent woman, in my opinion, and sees through the moral rhetoric to the real moves and

strategies in the values game. She is tired to death of all the moralism and the pietistic rodomontade that pervades the community
and epitomizes her aunt's attitude toward her and life. She cannot
bear all the conventional humility, the emotional, time-consuming,
and sexist moral calculus under which everyone operates. She is sick
of the respect and obeisance that she has been paying ever since her
aunt took her out of orphaned poverty, arranged a marriage for
her, and set her up in a house. She has no more gratitude left in her
at this exasperated point and she wants to withdraw from the
whole system. At this point she would rather be a hermit or a
witch, than carry the burdens and responsibilities of the system.

To be sure, she is not the only person who feels this way. People
do eye the possible exits from the value system, and the lexicon of
deviance recognizes and guards against this very fact. Clearly, the
community members cannot withdraw their commitment to the
community values, and, equally clearly, ways must be found to pre-
vent the opportunist or clear-thinking maximizer from withholding
his contribution to the moral order. The lexicon of deviance serves
this purpose. Women, whose commitment to the moral order is
critical, must be even more "closely watched" for deviationist tend-
encies. Therefore, the lexicon of deviance is more highly developed for them. The system of values and the conceptions of deviance define each other and, in so doing, declare what is admissible
and what is not.

DEVIANCE AND THE CONDITIONS OF SOCIAL ORDER

The way people think about good and evil mirrors their concerns
about the way the world should be ordered. Up to this point I
have used examples from the Zapotec moral canon to illustrate that
the Zapotecs define deviance in sociological terms and safeguard
the most important social matrix that orders their world—the network of categorical relations that I have called the inside.

Underlying the major value postulates of the community is a set of propositions about social relations that operates in a general way to ensure coherence of the social organism. The most important of these postulates is that of equalitarianism, or reciprocity. To put it in anthropological terms, these communities are systems of symmetric exchange (cf. Lévi-Strauss, 1949), which is to say that the social order is premised on and created by the reciprocal exchange of symbols between individuals and household groups. Daily acts of exchange create the social structure; exchange is the dynamic aspect of social relations. To return to the three general value statements that the Zapotec make, "humility" can be restated as a set of rules on how to engage in a relationship of reciprocal exchange; "trust" can be restated as the set of rules that enable one to be a partner to reciprocal exchange; while "respect" is a set of rules on how the social categories must be ordered so that the exchange is a general activity or the social categories can be kept in order so exchange can take place.

Once this is understood, we can turn to the lexicon of deviance and see how it facilitates exchange and how, in the realm of ideas, it implies an ideology that makes reciprocal exchange possible. I mentioned earlier that the definition of the good man in Zapotec (and probably throughout traditional Middle America) is "the man who knows how to do you a favor," and a favor is no more nor less than a unilateral act of exchange that carries with it the expectation of reciprocity. But direct preachments and admonitions are not the only way that exchange is buttressed in community ideology. The lexicon of deviance is so constructed as to facilitate conditions of exchange, and, once this is understood, seeming anomalies in Zapotec thinking about immorality become quite clear. One example of such thinking in the form of a question exemplifies this point: Why is it that the Zapotecs regard the "evil eye" in such a light way, but react very strongly to the social type whom they label "a person who is contemptuous of others" and "a censorious snob," or, in our vernacular, "a put-down artist."

When I did my first field work in Mesoamerica, in the Sierra de Puebla, I noticed that, despite the very poor health conditions and very high infant mortality rates, mothers of young children did not seem to fear the "evil eye" nearly as much as I felt they ought to, since the eye is responsible for sickness and sometimes the death of their children. The same was true in the Valley of Oaxaca. On the other hand, I was surprised in this research to see that the "judger," or the person who is quick to denigrate another, and the "contemptuous person" were so very high on the list (Appendix 1). The explanation for both these anomalies lies in the explication of the ideology of exchange.

When I asked the question about the "evil eye," the subjects understood that I wasn't talking about people who kill a pig or child with their baneful stare out of sheer malice. They understood that such people would be called witches; what I was referring to were people who unwittingly or unwillingly, or both, had the capacity to inflict illness on children and animals. They also understood that either it was very difficult to know whether someone had this capacity (according to some informants) or everyone has it at some time or other (according to others). Nevertheless, if I as an American father of three children were asked about persons who could inflict illness and death upon my children and destroy my most precious possessions, I would say that such people are very dangerous and best removed from society. I would probably make up some ideology about them that would ensure that neither I nor my suburban neighbors were so lightly placed in jeopardy of life and fortune. Not so the members of this community, and an examination of why this is so takes us further into community ideology.

The major occurrence of "evil eye" is when someone evinces envy at the sight of some other person's possession. For example, Wenceslau was clearly envious of the owner of a cow: "He wanted to buy this young heifer that had just arrived from the mountain. It was beautiful, and he wanted to give a bull in exchange, but the owner of the heifer refused. Wenceslau offered to throw in eighty pesos on the deal, but the owner wasn't interested. So Wenceslau threw evil eye at the young animal. And soon it was covered with fleas, and even though they bathed it with ashes, it never got better, and finally died." The owner could have sold the cow, which would have been doing a favor to Wenceslau; it is always, morally, a seller's market in the community. Then the cow wouldn't have died. The same kind of thing happened to Javier when his nephew remarked, upon seeing Javier's new cow, that it surely was a most magnificent animal. Javier sold it to him right away so that he wouldn't lose everything. He was angry about that, since he wanted the cow and not the money, but he had to sell it after his nephew had indicated his envy of the possession.

Why is it that if a person expresses a desire for an object or if he admires an object it must be destroyed or transferred to his possession? We should not think that the villagers are terribly altruistic, delighting in the unmotivated disposal of their possessions; they are not. The answer lies in the importance of the ideology of exchange between equals. Interaction is premised on the assumption that everyone is equal. And this equality is tangibly realized in the constant round of petty exchanges between neighbors and kinsmen. People are forever asking for favors from others, even if they have no actual need. The doing of favors is central to the value system of the community and is the act that creates the day-to-day system of social relations. Exchange symbolizes the relationship between people, as Eusebia points out in her usual pragmatic and realistic way: "Look, you give food to good people if you're eating, or even if you're not eating. But if bad people come, you don't give them a crumb, even if you're eating at the time they arrive." Refusal to enter into an exchange relationship is tantamount to an accusation. Local proverbs attest to this: "the person who doesn't do you a favor isn't a person to be trusted," "people who are deviant simply won't reciprocate a favor," and so on. The refusal to enter into an exchange is a gratuitous display of malice, because it is impossible to lose on an exchange since *everyone is equal in the community*. One always lends to others, and they always reciprocate. This is how trust is displayed and why one acts in a humble manner so as to maximize the communication of trust to a neighbor whom one respects, just as he respects his neighbor. Therefore, when a neighbor sees another's heifer or child and admires it, he unwittingly suggests that there is an asymmetry, or an inequality, in their relationship. One has something that the other doesn't. If it is a cow or an object, it is exchanged; a favor is done. If it is a child or an object that one is unwilling to exchange, the offending item must be removed from the relationship. It dies.

This explains, I think, why "evil eye" is not so bad after all. Clearly, any activity that results in the death of children and loss of valuable property is not good, but the "evil eye" is not nearly so bad as witchcraft. Why? Because witchcraft exacerbates the distinctions between people and impedes communication and exchange. Witchcraft could be seen as the act of the self-interested man, dedicated to a program of unconstrained maximization. In witchcraft there is no equilibration as there is when the "evil eye" breaks down the barriers to the free flow of exchange.

This emphasis on exchange between equals explains why the community members think the judger or put-down artist is such a serious deviant. These people fancy themselves to be in some superior position and derogate others to maintain it. Eusebia explains: ". . . like my *madrina*, for example; she has a rotten way about her. She's very selfish, and she's a real judger. She thinks she's got everything in the way of material things, and when she comes here we don't give her anything." That is, since she does not feel bound by the ideology of equality, then Eusebia's family does not even bother to engage in that important symbolic act that affirms equality; they do not do her any favors. Such people are removing themselves from the community and deserve condemnation and little pity. Eusebia illustrates how she felt about a contemporary of hers who was a real put-down artist at a time when she and her girlfriends were all feeling a little insecure about their place in the value system. They were thirteen and fourteen years old and were beginning to enjoy sex for the first time:

That girl . . . she always used to go around saying, "Look at those other girls; they want sex so much from the boys that they go from house to house asking to be laid. They are terrible people." She was always saying that about the rest of us.

But as soon as she got the chance she went to a boy's house herself and had sex, and, instead of coming home, she stayed there. And all the boy had to do to have sex with her was ask her and she'd do it. The boy's grandmother didn't like her, however, and threw her out of the house. She met up with another boy who was sixteen and could screw her beautifully, better and stronger than the first boy. She lasted a week with him and then a boy came down from [a town in the hills] and he was even better for her. Well, he took her off to Tapachula [a city by the Guatemalan border] and abandoned her there. God only knows where she is right now.

So much for people who try to put others down. If they explicitly deny the equalitarian basis of society, they deserve neither help nor pity.

CONCLUSION: DEVIANCE, REHABILITATION, AND SOCIOLOGY

This discussion may be difficult for North American readers because I have used case study data to make points about the relationship between meaning and society. We have a good deal of common-sense ideology about the individual and his psychological motives, and it is very hard to get across the idea that, when I am talking about individuals, I am not interested in them as people, but as elements of the social organism. A critical reader might well feel that the Zapotecs are not really as different from us as I have been suggesting. People have pointed out, for example, that we de-

fine mental illness sociologically as well. The case of parents bringing their adolescent child to the psychiatrist because the child
either has no friends or is unable to maintain decent relationships
within the family is so frequent as to be routine. A host of writers,
from Harry Stack Sullivan to Erving Goffman and from Jules Henry to Gregory Bateson, have insisted upon the interpersonal basis
of psychiatric conditions, schizophrenia in particular, and have
shown very clearly that it is sociogenic. Quite so, but the point is
that American society (and Western society in general) takes its
sufferers to psychiatrists, who have an expertise in intervening in
people's psychological problems. Goffman collected his data by
participant observation in a psychiatric ward and called one of his
books *Asylums*. We may recognize the sociological genesis of deviant behavior, but we also have a scientific and folk explanatory
model that puts the responsibility for morality and cure on the individual. This way of thinking is deeply rooted in Western thought.
It is certainly as old as Thucydides, who wrote 2,400 years ago and
was rediscovered and glorified in the Renaissance and the Reformation. But this is the point where the Zapotecs differ from us. They
define social conditions as problematic and ignore the individual.
To be sure, their moral canons have relevance for individual conduct, but the individual is not their concern. And this has nothing
to do with some culture-bound notion of the "worth of the individual," which used to distinguish enlightened Westerners from
benighted Easterners. It arises from the comparatively stable conditions of the Zapotec society and their long history of association.
One might think that any community with a history of eight centuries of stable association, where everyone was related to everyone
else in a multitude of ways, would be a community where people
knew each other intimately. Americans who have rural backgrounds
or come from small towns remember well the long evenings during which their parents and their grandparents talked about the
genealogy of personality and bared the skeletons in every neigh-

bor's closet, going back for generations. But the Zapotecs, as Oscar Lewis (n.d.) noted about his Nahuatl villagers, do not know each other very well. This is not because they are obtuse and unobservant; it is because it is unimportant. They stigmatize conditions under which it would be advantageous to know people well. If one had to know people very well it would mean that people were idiosyncratic, inconstant, moody, indirect, and changeable. Their expression "We see the face, but we do not know what is in the heart" is not an expression of despair. They do not have to know what is in the heart, because it isn't defined as being very interesting and it shouldn't have anything to do with human relations.

They do not, therefore, have to overcome their own prejudices about the character of people who go wrong. They know their own society and how it works, and they are aware of the sociological nature of deviance. They have no need to peer into people's hearts and minds and perceive strange motives and dark desires. Society must be maintained, and the rules of the epistemological and social order must be upheld, but the individual can be left alone. In the discussion of the most serious general deviant of all, the witch, we shall see that however much the witch may be the product of the social order, no one believes that he himself is a witch, and no one has to don a deviant identity. Durkheim was quite correct and would be comprehendible to the Zapotecs when he says that deviance is a necessary set of ideas for any society to ensure the boundaries of the moral framework. But the Zapotecs, unlike ourselves, have left the matter there, in the realm of ideas where it belongs, and they have not taken what to us is the necessary next step. They have not sought to extirpate evil by setting boundaries on the freedom of others and by driving them permanently to the margins of society.

This is abundantly clear if we look at the process of rehabilitation in the village, which is much more thoroughgoing than our own and succeeds not just in defining offenders as "ex-convicts"

who have "paid the price of their wrongdoing," but in obliterating
the crime itself. A sort of collective amnesia occurs, and people
deny that there was any kind of crime in the first place. I will
show later in the discussion of witchcraft that rehabilitation is not
necessary for most offenses in the village, because there is no public manner of labeling major offenders and people of one's inside
group will not accede to a deviant label in any case. But there is a
public process for the most serious crimes, which are dealt with by
the regional authorities and which involve modern judicial procedures. Murder is such an offense. There had been two recent
murders in the village when I started my field work, and I was able
to observe the process of rehabilitation.

The first murder took place in 1960. Joel and his neighbor had
not gotten along at all well. They had fought over the right of way
by their house and over other petty annoyances (wandering animals, for example) that arise between neighbors. The hostility
grew between them and rose to a head when the neighbor woman,
according to Joel's account, seeing Joel limping, taunted him by saying that she had given him his limp and was going to kill him by
witchcraft; after she had killed him, she was going to kill his wife
and then all his children. According to his own testimony, he was
frightened to death by these threats and together with his sons laid
plans to kill her. They waited until she was to go early to market,
ambushed her on the road, and chopped off her head with a machete. Joel was tried, convicted, sentenced, and served almost a
year in jail. The second murder took place in 1965. Conflict had
broken out between two groups over water rights in the upland.
The murderers laid an ambuscade to trap the victims and dis-
patched one of them in a fight. But there were witnesses, and as a
result the murderer was caught and convicted (as in Joel's case) by
the regional court in the market town.

Thus, when I arrived in 1965 two murders had occurred in the
past five years, and the two murderers were living in the village. By

the end of 1968, there were no murderers; the two men had not emigrated, but they had been deassigned, or unlabeled. In both cases the process was clear. After their convictions, they had both spent a short time in jail, and upon their return home they had been almost penniless (Joel more than the second murderer). Both had worked extremely hard regaining their substance. They had avoided people at first, but more and more, as a year and then another passed, they were able to restore something of their former economic position and to pay off the kinsmen from whom money had been borrowed for their fine. They reestablished social relations with more and more people and began to restore the network of relationships that had been disrupted by the murder and by their removal from the community. The unlabeling spread from the household throughout the inside group, with the offender acting as the moral entrepreneur. One cannot tolerate murderers in one's intimate group. If one engages in acts of exchange with a person and thereby admits him within the company of "those who live close to me," then one can hardly suggest that he is a murderer. If he is a murderer, then his friend is as well, because the act of exchange is premised on the categorical congruence of the two exchanging parties.

Joel was helped by the fact that he had four brothers and five children, all of whom had godparents, and it was comparatively easy to establish exchange relationships with them and with the close affines of his brothers. He was also helped by the fact that the woman he killed had no living husband and only one son, and he was comparatively helpless to counter the political move that Joel was making. Similarly, he made it clear that he would contribute what he and his family could to the community, and he actively showed that he was the humble, trustworthy, and respectful person that he had been before the murder. Within four years after his conviction for premeditated murder, he was holding a political post in the village, and, ironically, it involved looking after all the children during fiestas so that they didn't get obstreperous, hungry, or lost while some village event was going on. The sight of this convicted murderer, standing with his baton of office and herding a gaggle of toddlers, indicated more clearly than anything that he had been rehabilitated. He was no longer a murderer. Today most people will not even admit that he committed the murder. "It's a lie," they say. Only the relatives of the murdered woman, and in particular her son, still insist upon the label, and they are becoming more and more isolated within the community.

Rehabilitation consists not in the construction of some limbo status such as ex-convict, but rather in the declassification of the person entirely. We have similar kinds of mechanisms that are applied to middle-class or juvenile offenders, whereby we erase the judicial record after a probationary period is up, but we have the feeling that we cannot do this with felonious offenses and, in particular, felonies that involve serious harm to others. Yet, the villagers carry through the logic of their own pragmatic system, and in so doing they indicate how a complete rehabilitation is possible, even with the most serious offenders against the mores of the community.

4. Ideologies and the Definition of Sexual Deviance

U p to this point in the account of deviance in Zapotec, I have been able to cite the villagers directly in making my points about the sociology of deviance. They are perfectly conscious of the distinctions they make between kinds of behavior, and if trained (and pushed) they would come up with explanations not dissimilar from those I have produced from listening to them and from examining the way they talk about and arrange their thoughts on the subject of deviance.

From this point on, however, this method is no longer possible. Whereas (in anthropologists' terms) I have been developing the conscious model of behavior, when I talk about sex and witchcraft I have to go beyond what the informants say and postulate an unconscious model of what they would *have* to believe and act upon so that they could say the things they say and do the things they do. There are two kinds of difficulties with which every ethnographer has to deal. One is the difference between what people say they do and what they actually do, or what in anthropology is called the disparity between jural rules and actual behavior. They are related, but they are not the same thing. The second problem has to do with the reasons that they give for their behavior. Sometimes they know what they are talking about, and sometimes they don't. Sometimes they are quite unconscious of the "real" reasons why they act as they do, and it behooves us, if we are to understand the nature of deviance, to comprehend both the conscious formulations of the villagers and the unconscious ones.

In the next two chapters, I examine the conscious set of ideas about sexual deviance and witchcraft, respectively, and find that, however interesting they are and however much they give us insight into the way the villagers envision their social organization, they are not predictive in the slightest. If I thought that the villagers believe what they say, I would not be able to understand either the structure of their ideology or their patterns of behavior. Anthropologists, largely under the influence of Lévi-Strauss, have come more and more to see as their task the description of unconscious models of behavior and have taken the model of language as their guide. Conscious models, in Lévi-Strauss's (1953) terms, do not necessarily serve to explain ethnographic phenomena at all but rather to screen them.

The same themes that were observed in the study of values, kinship, and general deviance turn up in the study of sex and witchcraft at a deeper level. Once again, the study concerns the social order that underlies the ideas about sex and witchcraft, even though in both cases I outline what the conscious model looks like. In the case of sex, the conscious model inverts the value system that was laid out in Chapter Two, and I suggest that the inversion is a necessary release from the demands of the value system. In the case of witchcraft, the conscious model takes us into an examination of Zapotec cosmology and epistemology. In both, it is found that the Zapotecs cannot predict their own behavior with their own models, but that it is possible to do so by examining the sociological order.

Had I accepted the community ideology about proper and improper sexual conduct, I would have been led to make statements such as the following:

1. Sexual activity is supposed to take place only between men and women who are married in a monogamous union.

2. People are sanctioned (punished) for carrying on an extramarital affair. If a wife is caught, she is beaten by her husband; if it is the husband, he is warned, fined, or jailed, or all three.

3. Incest is defined as sexual relations between relatives up to and including first cousins, recognized relatives by marriage and fictives. It is abhorrent to the community and punished by the authorities.

The problem with these statements is not that they are not true. They are perfectly good translations of things that people told me about sexual behavior, but they raise more problems than they solve. For example, if all three statements were true, how would one account for the following:

1. The only person in the community who is not having, and has never had, an extramarital affair is considered a deviant. Hence, the one person who has actually followed the norm is considered a deviant.

2. There is no equivalence class that corresponds to our notion of adultery, despite the fact that it is supposed to be critical in the definition and discovery of deviant sexual conduct.

3. Gossip about sexual affairs is constant. Yet, the category of deviance that describes such activity is one of the highest on the list of deviants. The *wana bieha* informs on people engaged in illicit sexual relations to their spouses. Therefore, she is doing a good deed by upholding the morals of the community. Yet, in fact, she is universally excoriated and ranks as worse than a witch in the hierarchy of deviance. Why?

4. Incest occurs all the time. Sometimes it is chuckled over, sometimes it is treated as scandalous. Never is it actively punished.

5. If men beat their wives for reasonable suspicion of adulterous conduct, why is it that we come to know of so many cases in which the husband has had reasonable suspicion and has not beaten his wife. Our power to predict is minimal. Why? The same is true for the punishment of men for their affairs.

In order to explain the logic of the value system as regards sexual behavior we will once again have to ask questions about social categories and about "meaning" and once again be concerned with the basic, master distinction in Zapotec ideology, that between "inside" and "outside," or between "people who live near me" and "people who live far away." It is only when we realize that these distinctions are being worked out in the area of sexual behavior that the anomalies become understandable as part of the logical system of values that constrain sexual behavior. We shall see that "sexual intercourse" is a symbol that serves to define the "inside"; it relates a man and his wife (they can copulate), and it relates a man and his inner group of kinsmen (by virtue of the incest taboo). We shall see that so long as the act of sexual intercourse is confined to the "inside," so long as it stays where it belongs, extramarital sexual behavior is not actively punished. But when it goes beyond the inner circle, that is, when one forces his inner circle to expand its circle of "people who live close to them" and to alter its distinction between the inside and the outside, the apparatus of sanction is brought into play. In short, if one makes clear that he is symbolically including an outsider in the inside group and forces that knowledge on his kinsmen so that their distinction between inside and outside is confounded, the system is going to "get him" for it.

Let me first substantiate the statements I made about the anomalies in the system, by looking, first, at what upright, nondeviant sexual behavior is in this community. The community members recognize that their village has a moral history, and they have a quasi-mythical reconstruction that motivates their beliefs about proper sexual behavior. They feel that "things were better in the old days," that is, about fifteen to twenty years ago. (There is positively no indication that the frequency of extramarital intercourse was lower in that period, which I take to be what they mean by "better.") Premarital sex was minimized by marriage practices, however. Girls were virgins upon marriage because they had been living under the very watchful aegis of their mothers-in-law since well before menarche. Marriages were usually arranged, and the residential changes took place well before the age at which defloration could be seriously entertained. At the time of the bridal night, the groom's godmother (*madrina de bautismo*), or a chosen substitute, would enter the hut where the couple was sleeping and would inspect a white cloth that she had left on the sleeping mat. If there was blood on the cloth, she would exhibit it to the wedding party of kinsmen, *compadres*, and neighbors. If there was no blood on the cloth, the pots and dishes that had been given to the bride would be broken, and a big tureen (*apazle*) would be hung on the door or wall of the house with an ostentatious hole punched in the bottom. Girls were generally virgins, by all accounts.

This custom of child marriage is no longer followed, nor is child betrothal. The school and the church have both put pressure on the community to give them up. But there is still pressure on the girl to remain a virgin. She can lose her virginity and seek the hand of a man, but as Eusebia put it, ". . . the boys aren't going to want her. After all, she is a lost woman. Boys always want a fresh girl, one about thirteen to fourteen years old. They always want a girl who hasn't been screwed."

Selby.

But nowadays the boys don't get to marry girls until they're about eighteen years old. [This is an exaggeration; fifteen to sixteen would be more accurate.]

Eusebia.

> Look, if she's a serious-minded girl, she's still going to be a
> virgin and not screwed. But, if she has been already, they're
> going to find out, and then they always abandon her.

It is particularly hard on the girl whose betrothal is broken. Today, once a girl is sought in marriage, it is normal for sexual relations to begin, if they have not already; then, if the betrothal is
terminated, everybody knows the girl is no longer a virgin.

Despite the changes in custom that have taken place, the villagers relate, in the reconstruction of their past, how every woman was
a virgin upon marriage and was expected to confine her sexual activity to her husband, with whom she had grown up. Such an attitude leads us to expect that adulterous relations would be deviant
acts and therefore sanctioned, and in this the community members
will agree. They state quite clearly that the rule about sexual partners confines one to relations only with his spouse, but I know of
only one example where someone has actually followed the dictates
of the norm, and she is regarded as deviant. Guillerma was a four-
teen-year-old virgin at marriage, and she has never had sexual intercourse with any man except her husband. She has fulfilled the
village norm of propriety and rectitude, yet people regard her as
deviant, and it is interesting to try to discover why.

Guillerma is considered a deviant partly because of her illnesses.
She is sick a great deal of the time, from what cause it is difficult to
ascertain, although she and her family are convinced it is witchcraft. Her symptoms are those of migraine headaches. The headaches, which are crippling in intensity, began seven years ago,
when her husband left her for another woman. He was having a
discreet affair and she found out about it and became very angry
and accusatory. He left her and went to live with his new sex
partner.

He was right to be angry that she had been insufferable about a discreet affair. Guillerma had overreached herself and had acted out a lie. When Guillerma was married, her hand was sought by her husband's family, and she accordingly went to live with him. Later, her brother died, and Augustino (her father-in-law) permitted the couple to change residence. Thus, despite the fact that Augustino had sponsored the marriage, the residential arrangement was de facto matrilocal. Was it morally so? That is, did Guillerma's father have the right to invigilate her husband's sexual conduct as if it were a normal matrilocal contract? I think not. I doubt if Guillerma thought so either. Her husband regarded himself as eligible for the patrilocal prerogatives of greater sexual freedom and this necessitated further weapons on Guillerma's part. The sickness started. The illnesses brought her husband back and kept him at home, although they did not keep him from discreet affairs, which continue to this day.

When I say that Guillerma overreached herself, I am addressing a rather serious point. Norms are relative constraints; they are not absolute. Guillerma was acting as though the norm about sexual continence were a good deal stronger than it actually is. She overestimated the value of the norm that states that extramarital sexual activity is illicit, and, by using her sexual continence and virtue to castigate her husband, she put herself in the position of acting badly. The crux of her evil-hearted (deviant) activity lay in conveniently overlooking the fact that her marriage was not a matrilocal union, properly speaking, and the matrilocal privileges did not accrue to her. Thus, when she used the weapons of sickness and moralism to punish her husband, she was acting maliciously and not as a proper instrument of the system of values.

A similar example will clarify the point that the definition of normal and deviant sexual activity is partly a function of the interpretation of the relative efficacy of the norms and will assist in understanding how norms, definitions, and behavior interact in the system of action. Jorge and Santos both married matrilocally—their hand was sought in marriage by their respective fathers-in-law. Both Jorge and Santos are carrying on publicly known sexual affairs, but only Santos is labeled a deviant. In both cases the economic differentials for an acceptable matrilocal decision had existed when the marriage was contracted; that is, the wife's family was a good deal richer than the husband's, which in the eyes of the community offsets the shame of making a matrilocal contract. But the contract was abrogated in the case of Jorge, whereas it was not in the case of Santos. Jorge's father-in-law was openly exploitative of his son-in-law's labor, while consistently excluding him from the executive decisions in the household and denying him any discretion in the investment of the money that accrued from their joint ventures in milpa agriculture. The father-in-law is often cited as a good example of the "very stingy man," which, although not culpable in itself (except in the general sense of a person who will not do favors for another), is considered culpable if it excludes members of the immediate family from their allotted roles as decision makers. Jorge is bright, twenty-eight, and well into his majority. He deserves, by community standards, a major say in the investments of the household, and from this he is barred. Hence, in the eyes of the community, the contract has not been maintained; the father-in-law has abrogated it. Therefore, as far as sexual license was concerned, Jorge became eligible for the patrilocal prerogatives of discreet sexual liaisons. Despite the fact that his adventurings were more public and animated than should properly be the case, nevertheless, it was not he, but rather his father-in-law, who was judged to be culpable. In the case of Santos, the mother-in-law had provided him with cash and a house and had helped him in other ways. The contract was still in force. His conduct was therefore culpable under the contract conditions of matrilocal residence.

Thus, the definition of what constitutes deviant sexual behavior is partly economic and partly derived from social norms that constrain family formation. Any illusion that we may have entertained

about clear behavioral criteria defining sanctionable adulterous behavior is banished, and we find ourselves in the curious position of
knowing something about the criteria that are used to label someone a sexual offender (the matrilocal contract), but without any
clear idea of how one defines the deviant conduct in the first place.
Obviously, we are required to question the usefulness of the rule
that the informants give and are led to ask what the "real rule" is.
Finding the "real rule" will take us back to sociology and force us
to examine the relationship between social categories, particularly
the gross categorical distinctions between "people who live close to
me" and "people who live far away."

A clue to finding the real rule was discovered in examining those
occasions when active sanctions of wife beating or legal punishment
were administered. It was very clear that the community members
did not act according to the rule that every time a man had reasonable suspicion of his wife, or vice versa, he or she would be punished. Wife beating was much rarer than it should be by this rule,
and so was punishment of the male. In comparing the situations
where more or less public affairs were going on and wife beating
occurred and those in which it did not, I was forced to the conclusion that the critical variable that activated the sanctioning apparatus
was the identity of the person with whom the affair was proceeding.
If that person was "someone close to me," wife beating didn't
occur. When the person was "someone who lived far away," wife
beating did occur, despite the overlap between "people who live
close to me" and those jurally forbidden by the incest taboo.

One way of recognizing kinsmen or nonkinsmen is to have sexual
intercourse with them. The exchange of favors, usually small pres-
ents of food and drink between copulating couples, is an important
part of the act of sexual intercourse because it explicates and clari-
fies the favored relationship between the pair. It declares, as exchanges always do, that as far as each is concerned the other is a
member of the inner and not the outer group.

Sexual intercourse is a complex symbol in this sense. It relates categories of people, principally the inside and the outside. It is jurally reserved for spouses. It relates the categories of husband and wife in a positive way. In a negative way it defines the categories of recognized kinsmen. One recognizes those with whom one cannot jurally copulate, that is, those who are related by virtue of the incest taboo. But sexual intercourse can take place with practically anyone. Even incest by Zapotec definition is tolerable.

The offense that activates the apparatus of sanction lies in the elimination of the distinction between categories. In particular, it lies in bringing a person of the outside into the inner network of kinsmen. When people are on the outside, for all intents and purposes, they do not exist. They are unknown and unknowable, and although they can be malign (they are capable of witchcraft), they are "nothing to me." This is just as well, for, as we have suggested throughout this account, "my world" is a very crowded one. The Zapotecs live in an "impacted" village where they are related to everyone, where many people have interests in each other, and where they have to defer to those interests or at least take them into account. So much kinshipping is emotionally draining (remember Bi'či's explosion against her aunt). Maintaining the inside network with all the attendant favor asking and granting, trying as best one can to serve one's self-interest without recognizably impinging on others, and creating either new obligations or envy are all very difficult.

The major ritual and religious symbols of the society are built upon associations with "people who live near me," or insiders. This inside world is very crowded, and the villager's problem resides in the fact that, although he cannot exist in isolation, equally, he cannot tolerate the demands that a greatly extended kin group of insiders would put upon him. The rules of the kinship system act so as to permit the infinite extension of the villager's inside group, and his problem lies in keeping the number of ties that are actively pursued down to a reasonable number. First, the kinship system is open in the sense that the villager can extend the range of his kindred as far as he wants. The village is endogamous and has been for centuries, and as a result all are biologically related to everyone else. The Zapotec can activate those relationships if he wishes. Second, the rules of *compadrazgo* and affinal kinship leave the field open as well. The son of one's *padrino* is a *padrino* as well, as is his brother and his brother's wife. The tie can descend four generations in one's own line and in his family to siblings and their wives. The same is true for affinal kinship. A villager marries into a set of affinal categories that are theoretically capable of almost infinite extension. The grandfather of his wife is his *sagul*, so is the grandfather's brother and the brother's wife, and so can they all be to one's own brother and children. These are the very relationships that are the most difficult. They are kinship categories that demand a high degree of respect and trust. The symbols of kinship and the constraints upon interpersonal behavior can extend and intensify almost to the point of paralysis. Thus, each individual and each nuclear family must arrange their lives so that they can minimax to the most congenial degree; that is, minimize the number of ties necessary to maximize the level of security. It is a tricky tightrope to walk and requires careful control of one's behavior.

What happens, then, when a close kinsman of a Zapotec (his spouse) thrusts a new set of relationships upon him? He reacts by sanctioning this behavior and beats her or jails him because the delicate balance between insiders and outsiders is being decidedly shifted. Sexual intercourse is the symbol par excellence of the inside, and his spouse is introducing a new set of members into the inside without prior consent or knowledge. New sets of people who have interests in him and to whom he shall have ties and obligations are materializing because of the conduct of his spouse in openly carrying on with an outsider and converting him or her into an insider. The minimax solution is being abrogated by such behavior, and therefore he reacts by punishing the offender and publicly exposing thereby terminating the relationship.

But there is a second, perhaps deeper and more important, reason for a reaction to the public knowledge that one's spouse is carrying on an affair with an outsider. By confounding the distinction between insider and outsider, the offender attacks the symbolic order of society. The inside is defined by relation to the outside, and this distinction, which categorically dichotomizes the community, is a master distinction of the symbolic order. In the public recognition of an affair with an outsider, one is party to overriding this master distinction and thereby acting to subvert the symbolic system that alone makes society and self understandable and interpretable.

Two analogies from our own experience may be helpful. Burning the flag is an act that overrides the distinction between U.S. citizens, on the one hand, and "people of the other side," on the other. The act of burning the flag is an act that subverts the special, relativistically defined place that they reserve for themselves in the world, and thereby evokes a very strong reaction from the community, just as any other act of symbolic subversion would. Another analogy, drawn from the high school lore of a generation ago, is less global and more to the present point. Part of the lore that a high school sophomore and junior had to know in order to be men of the world concerned prostitutes. And one of the truisms that was purveyed by the knowledgeable was a rule that "you should never kiss a prostitute." Kissing a prostitute, for us, would also have been a symbolic act that confounded the necessary distinctions between categories of people. Kissing is an act of conjugal love, symbolizing diffuse enduring solidarity (borrowing from Schneider, 1968). It relates the categories of husband and wife or of boyfriend and girlfriend. In kissing the prostitute, one attaches this symbol to a relationship that is both temporary and concupiscent and that relates buyer and seller. One attacks the organization of symbols that makes the world of love, sex, marriage, and prostitution all understandable. The public recognition of an affair in the Zapotec community confounds the necessary distinctions between insiders and outsiders in an analogous way.

If we understand the meaning of the symbol sexual intercourse, the rest of the anomalies that were listed at the beginning of this chapter are resolved. Consider the problem of incest. I stated the range of the incest taboo. It extends to first cousins, second-degree affinals, and fictives at a minimum. A man of my acquaintance was having an affair with his cousin, and, although people would shake their heads, talk of incest, and cluck their tongues, they would also chuckle over it and speak in unhushed tones that indicated they were amused, but hardly shocked. The cousin was someone in the "inner group" who already had "interests" in the man and his kinsmen, should she have cared to activate them. She was activating them in the form of carrying on this affair, and, although this was wrong in theory, it did not call for drastic measures. The lightness of the offense was indicated by the exceedingly public way in which the affair was carried on. The couple knew that they were not courting disaster, and the suggestion that witchcraft on the part of the cousin might be activated to rid my friend of his wife was roundly scouted. There was no occasion for witchcraft; after all, she wasn't a person who "lived far away from me."

The fact that an adulterous relationship, if recognized, can be socially dangerous explains the very high placement of the *wana bieha* in the list of deviants. (She is fourth, even higher than the witch.) It seems counterintuitive that informants should place the "evil gossip" higher than the witch, but they consistently did so. The *wana bieha* is more evil hearted than the witch and much more so than the person who picks fights, or lies, or is abnormal. Her awesome malignity derives from the fact that she is a talebearer about sexual infidelities. She has supernatural powers to ensure that

her gossip is always believed, and she is mightily effective in pro-
voking conflict and undermining the categorical order upon which
social relations depend. Here is the *wana bieha* in action, in a folk-
loristic account that Santos furnished.

This is what a *wana bieha* did. In those [olden] times there was a
happily married couple. Now the devil is always very eager to gain
the souls of those who are happy, and this couple was living happily
and in tranquility . . . One day the devil came along and began to weep
because he could not gain the soul of a young woman who was so very
beautiful, so pretty—who was so beloved by her husband.

Then along came the *wana bieha* and asked him, "Why are you
weeping; what's the matter?"

And the devil replied, "I can't get a hold of the souls of those two
and I have to get my quota for my chief."

"Well, then," said the *wana bieha*, "don't weep any longer over that.
I'll just have to go to work in order that you can carry out your task."

Then the *wana bieha* went to the house of the married woman, and
she was as charming as she could be. She arrived at the house and said,
"How are you, daughter?"

"Fine, thank you, grandmother. Won't you come in and have a seat?"
She was very polite to the old lady.

"Aren't you very busy, my daughter?" said the old lady.

"Yes, because my husband is about to come home to eat."

"Of course. Your husband loves you very much, doesn't he?"

"Yes, he does."

"Well, then, when he comes there is something you ought to do so
that he will love you all the more. I know full well that when he comes
home from work he likes to make love to you. Now what you should
do is to grab the scissors and cut his beard when he lies with you."

She went out, and the young woman agreed with her plan. Then the
wana bieha went to the place where the husband was working. She
said, "Ah, my son, you are in a hurry in your work because you want
to go home and make love to your wife. Isn't it true that you always
make love before you have supper?"

"Why, yes, grandmother," he said.

"But you should be careful because right at this very minute your wife is plotting to kill you so that she can go to live with her lover."

"How is that, grandmother; how can it be?"

"When you are making love, she will do it," said the *wana bieha*, and then was gone.

The husband went home, and his wife asked him if he wanted to eat.

"No, let us go to our sleeping mat and make love."

And they went to the sleeping place and she gave him everything, and he kissed her, and they took their pleasure until the man went to sleep. When the wife saw that he was asleep, stealthily she took the scissors and knelt over him to trim his beard. But as soon as she leaned close to him with the scissors to cut his beard, the husband saw it, and he seized a great knife and plunged it into her breast and killed her.

The devil . . . was very happy now that he had gained control of the soul of the beautiful young woman, and he gave the *wana bieha* three pieces of cloth.

The *wana bieha* does more than gossip. She points out the adulterous relationship to the interested parties and identifies the person who was in the outside and is now encroaching upon the inner space. Her supernatural powers enable her both to know and to act effectively in informing others. It is bad enough that she identifies "people who live far away" and introduces them as insiders; even worse is the fact that sometimes there is no basis for the accusation. Sometimes there is no liaison, and the *wana bieha* acts out of sheer malice to overturn one's categorical and social world. Life is sufficiently complicated within the web of kinship and under the gun of subsistence economics without one's having to cope with fictitious, unjustified, and uninvited conflict.

Given this explanation of what is involved in sexual matters, one begins to understand another puzzle: the community attitude to "immoral earnings." If the rule about sexual continence were an absolute constraint and if wife beating and ill feelings arose each time one learned of the extramarital affair of one's spouse, why do Zapotec men rent their wives out, or, as they say, "sell" them. That this happens and that it is in no way neurotic behavior is quite explicitly stated by the informants. Eusebia states: "There are some men who sell their wives to their lovers. And when the other wife comes around and complains that her husband is stepping out on her, the husband pretends not to believe it and says, 'I can't start a big fight between me and my wife.' That's what he tells his wife's lover's wife."

An interview develops this theme:

Selby.

But doesn't the husband always know where the money comes from?

Eusebia.

Some men ask, but others don't bother. Once they've got something to eat, it doesn't bother them.

Selby.

Well, you'd better give me an example.

Eusebia.

If there was someone who was very lazy and didn't care to work at all, and he still eats, then it's fine with him.

Selby.

No, an example from real life.

Eusebia.

Adam used to be very poor. He used to make charcoal a lot. [Making charcoal is a long, difficult, dirty job, very lowly regarded, and only resorted to by the very poor. It requires the man to spend a lot of time away from home working in the mountain. It takes from two to three days to make and the occupation has very low prestige.] He was really poor; he didn't have a burro to carry his charcoal, but used to have to carry it on his own back. But ever since his wife began to carry on with other men, she's earned three, five, or even ten pesos at a time; and they started to buy pigs, and then they sold the pigs and bought a cow, and now they have some resources. And the woman earned it all. They have land, first-class land in alfalfa, and Adam doesn't have to work anymore; he hires a hand to work for him. He has two milk cows and grosses thirty to forty pesos a day.

Not that this is a frequent occurrence; it is not. But the example and the practice point out the underlying rule that, as long as the individual with whom sexual intercourse is taking place is either not identified or of the inside, he does not impinge upon the interests of the group of near kinsmen and therefore is not a threat to the economic, psychological, or symbolic security of the group.

This also explains why wives arrange affairs for their husbands under certain conditions. Men require regular sexual outlets, for such is their nature, and if a man cannot be satisfied at home, outside arrangements have to be made. Once again, as long as the relationship is not recognized, no harm is done. Take, for example, the well-known story about Ulrico, who has been having a liaison for some time with Catarina:

Jorge.

> Catarina has her lover, all right. It's Ulrico, who is married to Alejandra. As a matter of fact, they're chatting right now up on the hill there. His wife doesn't say anything even though she knows that he's going with Catarina. Catarina thinks it's a fine arrangement and leaves meat [i.e., presents] for him in the full knowledge that Ulrico is happy about it. In fact, it was Alejandra who suggested it, saying, "Look, wouldn't it be better if you got yourself a woman, with me sick and all?" He didn't have anyone to wash his clothes even.

Selby.

> So Alejandra is quite happy about it?

Jorge.

> Sure she is. [She says,] "That's fine that you have a mistress because I'm sick a lot." Ulrico is happy as well, now that he can go out with his girl friend. He can sleep with her—not in her house, of course, because she has a daughter. And so they have sex in the fields and down the *barrancas*, and everybody seems pleased with the arrangement.

Such satisfaction in business arrangements, which rectifies an impaired family relationship, would be impossible if the constraints on sexual activity were absolute. They only make sense if we construct an unconscious model of what constitutes the deeper social and moral reality for the Zapotecs.

This model accords with what we have been led to expect from the discussion in the previous two chapters. It also fits in with the discussion in the next section of how witches are selected. It agrees with the repeated observation that the Zapotecs "think sociologically," that morally they are preoccupied with the conditions that bring about the social order. It is not surprising, then, that the act of sexual intercourse, that elementary act that creates and symbolizes a primary human relationship, should encode, as well, their preoccupations about the larger social order in which the symbol is embedded.

THE SEXUAL DRAMA: INVERTING THE VALUE SYSTEM

Although the unconscious model has explanatory power for us, it does not for the villager, who is largely unaware of the discriminations and distinctions he is making when he deals with sexual deviance. On the conscious level he feels that he is merely on the prowl for sexual liaisons, and not infrequently successful. If we look at the way he thinks about extramarital sex and goes about seeking sexual partners, we can see that in this microcosm of life he is inverting the value system. Just as the roles of master and slave were inverted for the Saturnalia, and just as Carnival marks a time when moral rules are suspended, changed, or inverted, so too in the village outright individualism, aggressiveness, initiative, risk taking, and ambitiousness are seen in the quest for sex. Humility is not a successful personal front; brazenness succeeds more often. The careful cultivation of trustworthiness gives way to machination and conniving. The manipulation of symbols so as to raise the self-esteem of the other person is replaced by a considered selfishness whereby one tries to get as many sexual partners as possible. In sharp contrast to the way in which interpersonal relations are normally carried on, the quest for sexual partners is carried out with bravura and suspense. The villagers recognize that overall low-risk strategy, with an associated low payoff, is appropriate for everyday (nonsexual) encounters, whereas a high-risk, high-payoff situation is more appropriate for the sex game. The risk is high because sexual activity breeds conflict, and sexual delicts are more likely to bring about punishment than delicts in the interpersonal game. Controls on sexual behavior are stronger and more frequently invoked than the controls on the interpersonal game.

First, it should be mentioned that everyone in Zapotec is capable of sex. The villagers cannot entertain the possibility that a man or woman would be impotent or frigid, unless they had been interfered with by witchcraft. Freud, as I mentioned, has not arrived in traditional society. Indeed, we can go further and state that the fact that intercourse takes place is meaningless. There is no notion analogous to the "stud" of our milieu—the genitally well endowed male who is capable of a large number of orgasms in a short space of time. This sort of behavior is simply not marked or recognized in community culture. Sexual intercourse from arousal to orgasm is regarded as natural and as automatic as breathing. "Men want intercourse with women, that's the way they are, and women want to have men too," and "People are always on the lookout for sex" say two proverbs. The following is a conversation with Eusebia on this subject:

Selby.

> Is it the younger people, in the main, who go out looking for sex?

Eusebia.

> Young people do it a little more, but everyone is looking for sex. If they have money they're looking for sure, but even if they don't have money, they'll still try.

Selby.
> But why do they? I mean, they have a wife and all.

Eusebia.
> That's the way people are. They always turn out like dogs.
> That's what we call people who are looking around for sex:
> dogs.

The natural act of sexual intercourse is strictly defined. Fellatio and
cunnilingus do not occur. For "natural" sex, the man emplaces himself on top of the woman face to face, and there is little foreplay.
Clothes are worn, not surprisingly, since privacy is very hard to
obtain, particularly if one is copulating on the family sleeping mat
with the children under the same blanket. The rear position for
male entry is utilized in passing encounters and is held to be highly
exciting. Men reportedly find the presentation of the buttocks very
arousing and they reach orgasm very quickly. But its use is confined
to passing encounters, and it is not known whether the excitement
derives from the sexual arousal at the sight of the female buttocks
or because the encounter is fleeting and, by implication, dangerous.

Although there are no points to be gained for reaching orgasm
or for merely performing the act of sexual intercourse, there are
points to be gained for inducing partners to have sex with one. This
is a very popular game that involves a wide range of emotional responses; it is a central focus of interest and concern for the community members. They, after all, are unaware of our unconscious
model. They think that their conduct is interpretable in terms of
their own ideology—ideology involving fear, rage, jealousy, anxiety, and passion in the search for sexual experience.

Men do get jealous when they discover or suspect that their wives
are having affairs with other men. Sometimes they beat them, as
we suggested, or have them put in jail, and the wives do likewise.
Similarly, men and women do feel "crushed" when they are unable
to carry off a desired liaison. A rebuff is dangerous and threatening
to one's self-esteem. One invests as much, or more, in the approach

to a potential sexual partner as in the act of borrowing money. And one is equally open to a rebuff that is so destructive to one's self-esteem. For this reason the overtures to a sexual encounter are well patterned and clearly indicated. Any reciprocal act of the exchange of valuables is tantamount to the acceptance of a proposition. "Women do not have any vices," goes the proverb, "because they do not go out into the street." They do go out, but their conduct is demure, and they are careful not to talk to nonkinsmen or those distant enough so that sex would not be incestuous. Should a woman speak in any kind of animated fashion to an eligible male or should she accept any kind of gift, the understanding is given that she will have sexual intercourse with him. Teasing a male is a dangerous business. It leads to misunderstandings and bad feelings and a humiliation that will require some act of vengeance on the part of the male. The scale of vengeance is related to the severity of the humiliation and the degree to which the male interprets the humiliation as being a wanton affliction on the part of the female. It can be mild, as in the following account where the male was responsible, at least in part, for his own failure:

Not long ago this young woman took a lover, and it turned out that the young man was extremely poor. But, nevertheless, he got caught up in an affair with this woman and promised her all manner of things. He made a commitment to clothe, feed, and look after her in any way she wanted.

One day the young man decided to go to the market town to sell some ploughs that he had made, and he said to her, "Let's go to town tomorrow; as soon as I sell the ploughs, we'll meet in the market."

The young woman accepted, and so the next day the young man took off for the market to sell his ploughs. Afterward, they met and he gave her all the money he had made. Then she went off to market and bought all manner of foods. She invited the young man to her house for eight o'clock [knowing that] her husband had stayed in the mountain to make charcoal.

So he arrived at the appointed time and sneaked around the back of the house and peered in through the bamboo to make sure that she was alone. And while he was making sure, her husband walked in.

"Hello there," said the husband to his wife.

"Hello, you've come home."

"Yes," said the husband.

"That's fine. Look, I went to town to buy all the things we needed because we were out of everything, and I managed to borrow some money to pay for them."

All the time the poor lover was stationed at the back peering in through the wall. And the wife was serving her husband a fine plate of food, and while he was eating, the wife slipped out to the back and said to her lover, "Wait a little bit until that man goes to sleep. I know he'll sleep because he's terribly tired from work, and then we can talk."

But the husband rather overdid himself at supper and, as pork is very "fresh" [i.e., a cold dish in the hot-cold syndrome], he began to feel a little ill. At the same time the dogs started to bark, and the lover took himself off and sat down in a little *barranca* [to hide from the dogs and people]. But the husband got worse and soon had a case of diarrhea, and he went to relieve himself into the very *barranca* where the lover was hidden. He bathed the entire body of the lover in shit. The poor lover had to leave for home.

When he got there . . . he got his wife up and changed his clothing, but he never could get rid of the stink.

Anyway, the next week, since he was still disgusted with the woman, he went with her with two ploughs to town. He sold the ploughs and went around the market and bought all the things that they had bought the week before. She walked along behind him, hoping all the time that he would give her the money, but he never did. He took all the things that he had bought home to his wife and children, and she went home with a basket as empty as it had been when she had left.

And that's how it was that she got her comeuppance from him. He got his vengeance in love.

This was a mild affront to the male. Had the understanding been more firmly made or had the woman been more of a tease, the humiliation would have been clearer, and more stringent measures, such as thievery and witchcraft, would have been called for. In one very low-key sexual liaison between siblings-in-law, it appeared to the male party, at least, that understandings had been reached, but despite his insistence on completing the bargain, the sister-in-law teased but did not allow him to have sex with her. In humiliation, the brother-in-law attempted to salve his *amour-propre* by stealing a *metate* (grinding stone) and a pig from her. He was apprehended on both counts, fined, and sentenced. The community reaction was interesting. He was censured, not for the attempt to have a sexual encounter with an affinal, but rather for his stupidity in attempting to steal this kind of property: a *metate*, which was easily identifiable and therefore exceedingly difficult to fence, and a pig, which was of sufficient value and importance that its absence would be quickly noticed and its disposal exceedingly difficult.

When he came before the Presidente Municipal, his defense was simple. The sister-in-law owed him the money and was unwilling to repay it; therefore, he had resorted to self-help in order to recoup his lost investment. But, as everyone knew, it was not so much a sound investment, as a speculation. It was up to him to realize the return on the investment and to achieve sexual access to his sister-in-law. He had failed to do so, and the lesson is clear: a fool and his money are soon parted. His defense was quite unacceptable.

In the heightened drama of sexual questing, *amour-propre*, self-respect, and dignity are more in jeopardy than in practically any other activity. The stakes are high, and the punishments stern. It is believed that witchcraft is very possible when a liaison is discovered; and the fact that one is gambling one's life or well-being in the search makes it all the more exciting and dangerous.

Self-help for an injured party can take other forms as well. There is one case of a killing and another of a maiming that "actually" took place. But, interestingly enough, in both of these "actual" acts of vengeance, the victim was not one of the lovers, but rather the informer, the person who pointed the finger at the cuckold. This is in line with community feelings about the relative offensiveness of the *wana bieha*.

By far the most frequent form of vengeance is witchcraft, and one can find every combination of attempted murder through witchcraft: mistress tries to murder wife, lover tries to murder husband, mother-in-law tries to murder prospective daughter-in-law, wife tries to murder husband, husband tries to murder wife, and so on. Every configuration of the eternal triangle is a potential conspiracy, according to what the villagers say. It sometimes happens that such powerful sanctions are activated for mere suspicion that a liaison is taking place. Or, in an extreme case, one puts one's life in jeopardy by hinting at a suspicion that he harbors about his spouse. Amelia reported the following extreme example:

One evening Joselita said to her husband: "Go, fetch some firewood, because there isn't any for me to make breakfast."

And the husband replied, "I'll go tomorrow morning first thing." And he left before sunup the next morning. He got the wood, and when he got back his wife wasn't in the house. "Where's my wife," he thought to himself, and he came and asked me.

Well, I said, "I don't know, because she was there a short while ago." He pointed out that the dough was ready for making tortillas, but the breakfast had not been made.

Well, the poor man had to be content with a cold tortilla, and he was still eating around ten o'clock when his wife arrived.

"Where have you been?" he demanded.

"I just went on an errand to my aunt's house," she replied.

But seeing he knew she plays around a lot with the men, he began to beat her; he seized a sturdy pole and really gave her a beating.

And after dinner—God knows what she gave him to eat—he died. She killed him within two days of the beating. The thing was that when he was angry she poisoned him by feeding him chile, and pork, and beans, and all the things that you are not supposed to eat when you are angry, just as the doctor tells us.

It is clear from the statements of the community members that the search for sex is one of life's great pleasures and excitements. Village life is boring. "There is no movement here; life is sad in the village," say the villagers in acknowledgment of this fact. One of the few recreational activities that exist is the search for sex, and spice is added to this potent brew by the danger involved. One can lose one's life and fortune or one's sanity in the chase. The search for sex, however, is played out on the same stage as that of everyday life. It utilizes the same symbols, but it inverts emphasis. It is an act of exchange, but without the sure expectation of reciprocity and with none of the moral gravity that marks the exchange of favors in everyday life. Everyday life has a low payoff. One works long hard days in the milpa, and one acts with care and circumspection toward one's fellow kinsmen. One adopts low-risk strategies consistently. The sex game is the opposite. One plays with high risk, and the payoff is also high. Perhaps we would be justified in saying that the careful tone, the meticulous balancing of accounts, the elaborate time- and emotion-consuming talk, and the staid conventions that bind exchange in the everyday world are only possible because there is an outlet, a mirror opposite, in the sexual sphere. The community members could not have the psychological stamina to carry on in the manner they do without the leaven of the quest for sex. If we put the question to the villagers they might well endorse our thoughts, but whether they would see the implicit irony is not certain. And the irony is that their culture, their style, all that makes them different from the rest of the world is premised on an activity that their value system declares to be deviant.

5. Witchcraft in the Community

In the next two chapters I want to examine the process that is central to the interactionist position in studying deviance: the process of labeling offenders. The discussion is a test case of the interactionist position that offenders are not people who have committed some well-defined deviant act, but rather people who have successfully been labeled by moral entrepreneurs and sanctioned. I consider witchcraft in this community to be a test case because I think I forcefully argue that deviance is not an inherent quality of behavior but rather the outcome of a labeling process. Witchcraft is a major form of deviance in the community, and there is no doubt in the villagers' minds that witchcraft takes place. But, in fact, as we know, it does not exist. In our positivistic or scientific view, witchcraft cannot exist as an explicit behavioral syndrome that can be unequivocally recognized, defined, and demonstrated by the people of the village. Moreover, there are no witches in the village. There are curers, to be sure, and the villagers say that "sometimes they are witches," but there is no one in the village who performs witchcraft either by sticking pins into dolls or by pouring mescal on the ground and muttering incantations. If we note the process by which witches are labeled and find that it is quite similar to the way in which offenders are labeled in our own society, it would seem that we are demonstrating that the process of labeling deviants has a reality of its own, quite apart from the objective facts of social life.

The same social processes that create the community and that guarantee the conditions of the social order create the witches as well. The labeling process that I examine in the next chapter is a collective act of negotiation of the boundaries of the inside and the outside. Witch labeling is the dynamic aspect of the creation and maintenance of the social boundaries, just as wife beating is. But witch labeling is constant and generalized, while wife beating is sporadic and directed at single pairs of people. Once this is understood, there is no question as to whether witches and witchcraft are good or bad, so long as witch finding or some analogous process exists. The process of labeling a witch activates social networks. In particular, it involves the central value of the insider group, that of trust. To communicate the identity of a witch is a singular act of trust. To believe the news is equally an act of inclusion. One does not communicate such dangerous news to strangers or to people who live far away. They are the witch candidates. As the news passes from household to household, or even within the same household, the boundary between the inside and the outside is affirmed. The acceptance of the witch accusation is tantamount to denying that the accused could be a member of the inside group, and as a result the bonds that bind the insiders are drawn ever tighter. With some few exceptions (which I will call "core" witches and discuss below) the identity of the witches is constantly shifting, according to the dynamics of the social order. But the process is constant. Ultimately, it does not matter who the witches are, as long as there are witches.

First I wish to sketch the current social science explanations of witchcraft, and then the native explanations. I will conclude this chapter by pointing out that they are closely related and that social scientists, by and large, have tended to rationalize the local ideas about witchcraft in terms of the scientists' own prevailing folk model. Four kinds of explanations are given for witchcraft in social anthropology. Three of them are functionalist, and one is based on social structure. Basso (1969) has summarized the literature on witchcraft and drawn upon the work of Walker (1967; n.d.). I would like to discuss first the social psychological explanations of witchcraft. In many traditional societies (as in this village) there is a great emphasis on harmony, orderliness, peaceableness, and nonaggressiveness. But, since people do feel antisocial emotions, some outlet must be culturally formulated for their release. The accusation of witches serves as an outlet for the individual to vent his feelings on a convenient scapegoat. Witchcraft functions in this context to deflect antisocial aggressiveness from the inner group, where it can do irreparable harm to social relations. Basso (1969) notes that Evans-Pritchard (1937) has found this explanation useful in Azande (Africa), as have Hallowell (1940) in examining the functions of witchcraft among Salteaux (North America), and Opler (1946) among the Chiricahua Apache (North America); and it is becoming increasingly more popular in African studies (cf. Tait, 1963, and Levine, 1962).

A second kind of functional explanation can be called the "behavioral control" explanation, in which the witch and beliefs in witchcraft are seen to be part of the sanctioning apparatus of society. The child is told by his parents and educators that there are people who are bad and are to be avoided because they have supernatural power to harm others. The child's conduct is controlled in two ways: first, if he acts in a deviant way, these malign witches will get him, so that he had better stick to the social norms (cf. Spindler, 1952); or, contrariwise, if he doesn't behave himself, people will think that he is a witch and will punish him and isolate him the way the witches are punished and isolated. Honigman (1947), Whiting (1950), Beattie (1963), and Walker (1967) have found this kind of explanation useful in their studies of Kaska (North America), Paiute (North America), Bunyoro (East Africa), and Nez Perce (North America), respectively.

A third kind of explanation is more sociologically based and suggests that in times of rapid social change, or social disequilibrium, witchcraft accusations will arise as a result of individual tensions and anxieties. This explanation is more Durkheimian in spirit and reminiscent of studies of phenomena like the inverse correlation between the price of cotton and the frequency of lynchings in the American South. Bohannon (1958) has a particularly good account of such a process in Tiv (West Africa), in which he correlates economic and social conditions with the outbreaks of witch accusations, and Richards (1935) and Douglas (1963) have accounted similarly for witch hunts in Central Africa.

The fourth type of explanation is social psychological too, but it focuses much more clearly on the structural arrangements of social groups and outlines how customary arrangements in society may themselves generate tensions and conflicts that are converted into witchcraft accusations. Perhaps the best example of this kind of explanation is Nadel's (1952) analysis of Mesakin (Nuba Hills, Africa) witchcraft. In this matrilineal society, stresses arise between a person and his mother's brother over property rights. Both parties can feel threatened and humiliated because of the customary way that inheritance takes place. The Mesakin require that the mother's brother shall give up part of his property and cede his social position to his sister's son at a time when he (mother's brother) is still young enough (in his late twenties) to enjoy the exercise of these powers. In giving up the inheritance to his sister's son and retiring in his favor, the mother's brother effectively defines himself as an aging man no longer capable of exercising leadership. For these reasons he is loath to make the transfer of property (and other rights) as the custom requires. Until he does so, however, the sister's son cannot take his rightful place in society. Tensions lead to witchcraft accusations between them. This condition occurs in those societies where there are well-defined social categories, or groups, with competing interests. Marwick (1952:232) concludes his study of Cewa sorcery with the following summary:

Beliefs in sorcery are a means of formulating tense relationships. This statement holds whether we adopt the viewpoint of the people themselves and think in terms of the imaginary relationship between sorcerer and victim; or whether, as objective observers, we concentrate on the real relationships between accuser and alleged sorcerer.

What do the contexts . . . examined tell us about the ingredients in the tensions that are expressed through beliefs in sorcery? A common element seems to be competition for a highly valued goal connected with such fields of aspiration as leadership, property, love or tribal politics. Such competition can take place and can generate tension because of uncertainty or conflict, associated, perhaps, with a lack of clear normative prescription or definition of the situation in which it occurs. There may be conflict between the claims of a genealogical position and those of personal qualification; or a conflict between a headman's traditional right to dispose of his matrilineage's property and the claims of those of his followers who have gone to the labour centers, where they have been exposed to individualistic values, and who have contributed their earnings to its accumulation.

In this sociostructural view, society is seen as the "villain" in the sense that it is set up so as to produce conflicts between certain categories of people, and these tensions are realized in the form of witchcraft accusations and sorcery. This kind of explanation has been found useful by Firth (1936) for Tikopia (Oceania), Rattray (1923) for Ashanti (West Africa), Wilson (1951) for Pondo (Southwest Africa), and Leach (1961).

Monica Wilson (1951) has combined the sociological with the psychological viewpoints in her interpretation of the beliefs about witchcraft in two African societies, Nyakusa and Pondo. Nyakusa living arrangements bring about tensions between neighbors; witchcraft accusations are directed at neighbors. Nyakusa feast patterns underscore the symbolic importance of the sharing of food between neighbors. Witches are believed to be entrail-dwelling pythons who lust after and covet food. Pondo witch beliefs are preoccupied with sexual material. This can be accounted for by the far-reaching prohibitions that rule out sexual activity with a very wide range of classificatory kinsmen. The Pondo, in contrast to the Nyakusa, direct accusation against their affinals, with whom, like the Zapotec villagers, they live in close association. By examining the sociology of community life, Wilson is able to understand why accusations are directed at some people and not others. By looking at the differences in the major institutional forms of two not dissimilar societies she can predict the context of the witch beliefs.

Basso (1966, 1969) has developed a variant on the sociostructural theme, which is closer to my point of view. In studying twenty-seven cases of Western Apache witchcraft, he finds that it is important to discover the precipitating causes of Apache witchcraft. All informants agreed that it was "hatred" that brought about witchcraft accusations. He finds it useful to make three assumptions about witchcraft accusations: First, as suggested, witchcraft accusations stem from interpersonal tensions. Second, the society is composed so as to put categories of people into conflict with each other (as in Nadel's [1952] argument). Third, given no change in the sociostructural alignments of society, this form of accusation will persist, and a statistical count of witchcraft observations will locate the areas of tension. He notes, first, that a person in Apache society must have "power" in order to be an effective witch. Only people of a certain age class have power: those who are married and have achieved "mature adulthood." Second, witchcraft accusations are not directed at close relatives, but rather at a structurally defined "out group," and, since the society is organized on the basis of matrilineal clans and phratries, "out group" is defined as a "person who belongs to neither my matrilineage, nor my matriclan, nor my group of matriclans (phratries)." Third, he suggests that the accuser must see the accused as having access to scarce resources that the accuser does not have, and thereby denying the accuser a favor. His analysis of the cases bears out these explanatory principles in detail and suggests that a sociopsychological explanation based on a theory of the out group (or social distance) and socioeconomic distinctions is necessary and sufficient for the interpretation of an accuser/accused relationship.

Everyone who has studied witchcraft seems finally to indicate that the notion of "tension" is fundamental to understanding. They differ in the way that they account for tension, from the psychodynamic to the social psychological, but the research strategy is the same: find the areas of tension and they will explain the direction, frequency, severity, and so on, of witchcraft accusations. The data base for all the studies is almost the same. Informants are interviewed and the main question is narrowed down to be one of how to account for the relationships between individuals. This is in accord with the subjects' framework of analysis, as I show in the next section. But if witchcraft is a form of deviance, and if deviance is sociological in nature, then it must be wrongly conceived.

PEOPLE AND THEIR SOULS

In understanding how the villagers think about the relationship between witches and themselves, it is important to understand how they conceive of their relationship with the spirit world. Like all traditional peoples of Mesoamerica, the villagers have a complex set of ideas about the soul. In the village, people have two souls. The first is the Christian soul that represents the spark and breath of life and that leaves the body at death; the second is an animal familiar soul (*tono*), which is implanted in the fetus during the prenatal period. (For discussion of the belief in souls in Middle

America see Saler [1964] and Adams and Rubel [1967].) The *tono* is important to the understanding of witchcraft. First, if a *tono* is maimed or killed, the owner will be as well; this is often prima facie evidence of the occurrence of witchcraft. Second, in order to identify a witch, one only has to discern who has a *tono* of a large supernatural cat, because all witches, and only witches, have this *tono*. Obviously, the villagers have a very powerful explanatory device, and it behooves the ethnographer to find the empirical correlates of the beliefs about *tonos*.

Finding out about Tonos

How does one "know" whether one has a *tono*? One "feels" it or one doesn't (one informant admitted that he didn't "feel" he was anything), or one dreams it. "For example, a person like yourself," says Amelia. "You dream that you're in a *barranca* and you take fright because you fall on your head, and that's how you come to know what *tono* you have" (the imputation being that only an animal of some kind would be in the *barranca*). But it can well be that one has not "felt" or "dreamt" himself to be anything. Amelia hasn't: ". . . the funny thing was that I was born near the hills [where the *tonos*, or wild animals, live], and I don't feel myself to be anything. I don't feel I am [i.e., have] a *tono*," explains Amelia.

Tonos are important on some occasions, and it is particularly good to know what *tono* other people have, insofar as there is a belief that *tonos* congregate in groups and work together. One woman died, for example, because her *tono*, a snake, was foolish enough to attack her ex-lover and attempted to strangle him quite alone, without the help of her fellow snake *tonos*. The moral was quite clear: ". . . poor Aunt Merina! If she'd only stuck together with the other snakes, she would have been all right."

The importance of the *tono* comes partly from the fact that whatever happens to the *tono* happens to the individual. Augustino, for example, tells the tale of a drinking bout at his house: "Caballo's father was sitting here right on the porch, drinking, when all of a sudden he clutched his side and rolled over groaning. He hurt very badly below his ribs. The next day we went out and found a wolf that had been shot in the side. From that time on we knew that his *tono* was a wolf."

Soul-alter, despite its clumsiness, is a good term for *tono* because of the identity of the person with his *tono*. The person and his *tono* interpenetrate. Since death and illness may be attributed to the death or illness of one's *tono*, curing is often predicated on the belief that either the curer *has* the same *tono* as the patient, or that he has special power over that particular type of *tono*. People will agree in principle that there are ways of deciding what *tono* a person might have, but these criteria are confoundingly ad hoc and betray no systematic structure at the empirical level. Informants do not agree about what the behavioral correlates of having a *tono* are, or the criteria are so general as to apply to a whole set of *tonos*. "How do you know that so-and-so is a . . . [lion/tiger/coyote/leoncillo/cat/wolf . . .]?" "Because he eats a lot of meat!"

Nor is there agreement on what animals can be *tonos*. I retold a story that I had collected that was based on the presence of a buzzard *tono*, and the audience hooted. Buzzards weren't ever *tonos* to them, although the family from which I collected the story clearly believed they were. The fact is that when *tonos* are being identified in some context (illness, death) these criterial attributes are *never* used to make the identification. However much information on the phenotypical attributes of *tonos* is available in the cultural lexicon, it doesn't have much predictive value for the community members and therefore is by and large ignored. To be frank, the many hours of conversation that were spent on the criterial attributes of *tonos* seem, in retrospect, to have been wasted. The imaginative contributions of the informants have an aura of unreality about them. The informants seem to be saying, "Yes, there are attributes that we assign to these *tonos*, but really nobody pays much attention to them."

The Uses of Tonalismo

Tonos exist to be used. For the villagers, *tonos* are "there" in the cognitive and phenomenological world. They are a resource, an explanatory device, which can be called upon when necessary to resolve ambiguities and paradoxes. The precise correlation between behaviors of one and the other, *tono* and man, are neither necessary nor particularly useful; *tonos* reduce complexity and ambiguity.

Let us start with an example of the uses of *tonos*. Merina was a woman of about fifty-five years of age and in the prime of life. She was strong, "fat" (i.e., healthy and attractive), vigorous, and hearty, and in the spring of 1968 she died very suddenly. Her family was stunned and inconsolable. It simply seemed incredible that her time had come (that her destiny, or *suerte*, had decreed that she die so suddenly, so without warning). An explanation was demanded, and within two months (by the time of my arrival) one had been produced. Santos's version is presented below:

What had happened was that this poor lady had taken up in a love affair with Carnuto [a young man of twenty-eight years of age], who likes to have sex with older women and has made his way through life starting with nothing and now has managed to acquire a little bit of property. Merina was fifty years old at the time. But she had always eaten well and so she didn't look as old as that. She didn't even know how old she was. As luck would have it, she invited Carnuto to come and do some construction work on her house. It was during this period, in fact, that he fell in love with her. Well, after a while the work on the house came to an end and he had to find another job, this in the neighboring town. And so he abandoned the arrangement he had had with Merina and went to work.

Now Merina has the *tono* of a snake, and she kept herself hidden in a stand of *carrizo* [reed grass] with her other snake companions. And when Carnuto went by on his way to the next town to work, she would come out and try to wrap herself around his legs and coil herself around his neck and even to try to strangle him, because of the anger she felt at the fact that he didn't want her body anymore and didn't want to carry on the affair. Merina knew that he had taken up with another woman, who was also about fifty, who used to take his breakfast down to him—she used to take hot tortillas, bread, chocolate, cheese, soft drinks. Of course she liked chasing after him because when an old woman gets screwed by a young guy, the blood of them mixes and the old lady stays young, and the young man gets old very quickly.

In any case, Merina knew that Carnuto was carrying on with the other woman, and so her *tono* leaped out in front of him to bite him, probably to kill him. But Carnuto didn't run off; rather, he grabbed a stone and threw it at the snake and struck it in the head. With that one blow, the animal was stunned, and Carnuto ran to cut a piece of *carrizo* and began to beat the hell out of the snake.

Merina was very sick; then the *curandera* came, but everyone knew she was sick from her *tono* because she complained incessantly of headaches. Then, in two days, she died. At that time nobody knew what *tono* she had, but within the fortnight everyone knew that her *tono* was a snake. And they knew as well that Carnuto had killed her.

There was an old lady there attending her in her house after she had died, and she found out what had happened when Merina had been beaten with the stick. She said, "I only wish there had been about eight or ten of us then nothing would have happened to her." But it was Merina's fault because she came out of her hiding place alone; if there had been a lot of snakes, then Carnuto would have had to run away.

How these accounts come to be accepted is difficult to reconstruct stage by stage. The communicative process fosters more-or-less completed stories that graduate one stage into the other, and as the story takes on more and more details ("assimilates to the interests of the hearer" in Allport and Postman's [1945, 1946, and 1947] studies of the serial transmission of rumor), the earlier versions are superseded. It was not possible to get an informant to indicate clearly the various stages of the development of a story. The birth of one such story was observed in the summer session 1968. We can partially intuit the story-making process by looking at the series of events after a sudden death and the way in which it became a *tono* death, after initially being labeled a "natural" death.

Elpidia died suddenly in August. It was a Thursday, and the news was carried by 5:00 A.M. Friday to the neighboring house where I was living. I staked out houses in all of the major parts of the village, and a baseline of observation was completed by noon on Friday. During the morning the church bell had been tolling for the death, and so it seemed appropriate for people to be asked, "Why is the bell ringing?" (The sequence of questions was the same.) "She died? But . . . why did she die so quickly?" And the answer to this query was followed by, "But, weren't there any *signs* in her death?" That Friday morning none of the six informants felt that there was anything "supernatural" about her death. Replies were of the kind, "that was her destiny, her luck," or "she died from colic," or "it was the pain that did her in." By Saturday morning, however, it was being reported that when Elpidia's husband had lifted up her corpse to dress it for burial, all her teeth had fallen out, despite the fact that all she had consumed was a soft drink. The following guarded conversation took place between my *compadre* and me (taken from journal):

Jesús.	That was an unusual disease, wasn't it?
Selby.	What, Elpidia's?
Jesús.	Yes. Her husband told us this morning that he found all her teeth on the sleeping mat.
Selby.	I don't understand.
Jesús.	It's pretty funny [laughs]. The people say that it was because of her *tono*; she was a coyote or a wolf, they say.
Selby.	How can that be?

Jesús.   Well, that's the way her first husband died . . . suddenly!
Selby.   What *tono* was it?
Jesús.   She had the *tono* of a wild animal, and, you know, some-
              times they try to catch the animal by putting poison in the
              belly of a dead sheep or goat, and when the wild animal
              eats, he dies. You see, the coyote likes to eat the belly of
              the sheep or goat first, and that's what does him in! [He
              goes out.]
Selby.   [to Jesús's wife]. How did Elpidia die?
Guillerma. My father says that her father died the same way. Sud-
              denly.
Selby.   What *tono* was it, what *tono* did she have?
Guillerma. A wolf, I think.
Selby.   How do you know?
Guillerma. I don't *know*.

At 9:15 that morning, a young field assistant came to the house
to go over some data, and he did not "know" that it was a *tono*
death. But by 10:15, a young girl who lived up the hill at the other
end of the village reported: "Don't you know that Elpidia was
running around her house before she died; that's what her son told
me. My mother says that she died from her *tono*."

I went next door to Amelia's to ask her if anything unusual had
happened lately, and she said that it wasn't a *tono* death. But within
ten days Amelia was reporting that it was a *tono* death after all and
that people were hinting about witchcraft. Three of the six informants whom I consulted regularly believed that it was a *tono*
death. Unfortunately, it was time for me to return to the United
States, and the investigation had to be given up, but the process
seems clear. Creating a *tono* death is a collective activity that is
premised on the definition of a death as "unexpected" or "demanding explanation." A death demands an explanation when it occurs
counter to the *suerte* (destiny) that each person has. The presump-
tion of *suerte* is only made when a person is very old or has been

sick frequently with illnesses of God, that is, had been sick and was cured a number of times in the immediate past. A good proportion of deaths are attributed to *tono*. But whether the *tono* animal, and thus the person, has been killed by witchcraft is a separate process that requires further verification of the illness and the search for a witch.

WITCHCRAFT AND WITCHES

Although witchcraft can be involved in any sudden or unexpected reversal in one's fortunes, there is one context in which there is prima facie evidence of the working of witchcraft—when one is killed by an "illness of the people." There are two kinds of illnesses: "illnesses of God," which can be cured by either the doctor, the nurse, the curer, or all three taken together, and "illnesses of the people," which cannot be cured. Amelia explains, "If it's an illness that God has sent, then it is cured right away; a good disease is easily cured." Or, as she explains in another context, more fully:

A good disease is nothing to speak of. You get well fast with a pill, or you go to the doctor and he gives you one or two injections, and that's it. But if you get up the next morning and you're worse still . . . [then it's not a good disease]. From that point you get pains in your body all over, shivering fever, pain, lots of it, like someone hit you with a machete. You go to a curer, but you don't get well. Every time you are cured it gets worse and worse and worse. The medicine doesn't do you a bit of good; in fact, it makes the illness worse. And that's how it comes about that people believe that it isn't a good disease.

As Jesús puts it: "If it's a witchcraft disease, the doctor's no good, the nurse is no good, the curer's no good. Hell! Even the X-ray machine can't help you."

To be sure, this is not the only context within which witchcraft is to be identified, but it is by far the most frequent. Insofar as we are not interested in detailing all the "types" of witchcraft incidents but rather in constructing an account of the process of witchcraft and witch identification, we shall use illness and death as our explanatory focus.

If a disease comes about because of witchcraft, it is of both interest and importance to the villager to find out the motives for witchcraft and the identity of the witch. If he can discover what the motives for witchcraft were, he will have new insights into his social relations and social situation. An identification of the witch will enable him to take measures to neutralize the harmful influence and institute a rapid cure. Both kinds of investigation are carried on simultaneously, and the result is a reassessment of his own conduct and his interpersonal world.

Two very general, and simple, statements can be made about the situational context of witchcraft activity in the villagers' ideology. Witchcraft emanates on the psychological level from "institutionalized envy," to use Wolf's (1955) term. Envy in this subjective sense comes about in part because one has exceeded another's expectations in his acquisition of values, be they money, happiness, health, or property. Unlike Foster (1967), we need not presuppose that there is a generalized notion of balance or "limited good" shared by all community members; envy is a relative thing. A person may come to display envy because his own fortunes have sunk, rather than because his neighbor's have risen. There is a convenient ambiguity here: "I [the villager] am the judge as to whether some other person has changed his situation such that he will envy me and therefore view me as an appropriate object of witchcraft." A typical decision could be phrased in the following way: "Juan has had a bad year in his farming, whereas we have done 'average.' Therefore, Juan envies us, and, therefore, we think that he is capable of using witchcraft to right the balance between us. Therefore, Juan is a witch."

The use of envy as a stereotyped explanation for witchcraft is foreign and frustrating. It was in the interviews about witchcraft that I encountered the sociological thinking of the Zapotecs. I found that I could not get any kind of introspective explanation from the informants. Stories are told, and told with drama and detail, but close inspections of the motivations of others are completely absent. Psychoanalysts in our society might say that the villagers are rigid and highly controlled, that they are fearful of others, and that they interact in standardized and conventional ways. They might be called antiintraceptive in Murray's (1938) terms, or not at all psychologically minded. One might hypothesize that close inspection of the villagers' own motives would involve them in an examination of unconscious material and processes in their own personalities, which in turn would raise such anxiety that they suppress and deny impulse.

But, as I have suggested above, this kind of an explanation misses the point. Envy is a personal reaction to a shift in the social order to one's disadvantage. The major generalized form of deviance—witchcraft—reflects what the domain of deviance reflects as a whole: a preoccupation with the way the social order is constituted or with the rules that relate social categories. The notion of personality does not have great explanatory value for the villagers. Gearing (1970:137–138) has noticed exactly the same thing among the Fox Indians and explains it as follows:

Human cultures are able drastically to mold experience, to draw one dimension of reality into sharp relief and suppress another. Our contemporary Western life draws into sharpest focus the birth and continuing flow of experience and the resulting personal qualities of mind of individual human organisms; when we meet another we want to know where he has been, what he has done, what kind of man he has become, and where he seems to be going. As for that other dimension of reality, enduring organization, we of course must continually act in its terms and are therefore aware of it at some level of mental activity. We think often, for example, of those aspects of organization that affect and express ranked status. But it seems that we rarely think about enduring organization with clarity and direction and completeness, except under special circumstances (as when we are required to describe the table of organization of a factory). To appear to think consistently in everyday life about one's social positions and the positions of one's fellows seems, to us, a little indecent.

For the Fox, the emphasis appears to be reversed. The primary reality habitually considered with full awareness by a Fox, somewhat systematically and with clarity and direction, is enduring organization. A Fox, I think in retrospect, sees another most concretely and precisely when he views him as an incumbent in a social slot, sees himself moving into the slot, occupying it at the moment and acting appropriately or not, and moving out. Primary Fox reality is, I believe, such a system of social positions that endure. I think of my friend: "Joe (who is a father) . . ." A Fox thinks of his friend: "This father (who is Joe) . . ."

So it is with the Zapotecs. Each one of the eighty or so cases of witchcraft I recorded was attributed to envy, that is, a reaction to a shift in the social order. The people see witchcraft as emanating from envy and as precipitated by an incident of conflict, but not all conflict precipitates witchcraft. To generate a witchcraft explanation the victim has to fall ill and must have a serious illness that cannot be cured by the means that identify a "good" disease. Given that conflict arising out of envy has eventuated in an illness "of the people," the next problem is the identification of the witch.

IDENTIFYING THE WITCH

When I began this study I thought there must be some criterion that the villagers used to identify a witch on behavioral grounds. It seemed "obvious" or "commonsensical" that, if the witch role was consistently assigned to the class of deviant behaviors high on the rank orderings with "murderer," "abortionist," "thief," and "supernatural gossip," and if all these had clearly distinguished attributes, then "witch" would as well. For this reason a great deal of time was spent inquiring about the character and lifestyle of purported witches, as well as about the way I could unambiguously tell their *tono*; and a great deal of time was wasted. It became clear that there was neither a stable set of personality characteristics that implied the role label "witch" nor any observable behavior that could be identified as witchlike and would lead to the appropriate use of the witch label. The following question elicited little consistent data: "Look, I'm new around here, and I have two children and I worry about them. Now I know that the witches can get my children, so please tell me how I can tell who the witches are!" Informants whom I knew well were sympathetic and went to great lengths to tell me that I could rely on them, but they could not produce anything like a stable list of criteria for identification. After every identification the informant was asked, "How do you know he is a witch?" And the disappointing fact is that the criteria were hopelessly muddled and ad hoc. Jesús pointed out why, when we were discussing one person who many thought was a witch. "He [the witch] always behaves well with his neighbors and family. He never gives any demonstration of the fact that he has an evil heart. He never has fights with them. We can see his face, but we never know his heart. He's a good citizen. He always gets along well with everyone. If it's possible, he makes good friends of those he intends to bewitch. Witches never pick fights and they never tell about themselves either." In fact, as Jesús points out, bad behavior doesn't lead to a witch identification at all:

Selby. What about a person who acts badly, fights and makes enemies, behaves badly with his neighbors? Do the people say he is a witch?

Jesús. No, they don't name him a witch; they just say that he's an angry person, or a person who likes to fight.

Local Methods of Identification

Witch identifications are, of course, reconstructions after the event, the event being the identification and labeling of a "bad"

sickness. According to community ideology, help and information
for making identifications can come from four sources: dreams, an
analysis and reconstruction of "suspicious encounters," an analysis
of motives for the bewitching, and the curer, who will hint at or,
more rarely, give the identity of the alleged witch.

Dreams as Diagnostic Criteria. The actual identity of the witch
may not be clear from the data in a subject's dreams alone; it is
possible that the only information conveyed is that witchcraft is
taking place. This is particularly true when one dreams of the out-
size "cats"—the *tonos* of witches. Amelia reports of an actual
identification (when her husband and his mistress were conspiring
to kill her): "When you dream of these cats, and I say it [as one]
who knows because it has happened to me, you dream that they are
grabbing a hold of you and squeezing you tight. Then witchcraft
is going on. 'I can't endure it,' you say; 'I can't take it. I'm frightened, and I want to grab it; I want to run, but I can't find the
strength. I'm tired, tired, and I don't make a run for it, and the
cat won't let me go . . .' "

Sometimes the dreamer *can* identify the person who is carrying
on the bewitching, if the dream conveys sufficient information.
Santos gives an account that contains all the elements of a routine
witchcraft case:

Selby.　　How would I know if a person were a witch?
Santos.　　You know right away, because you dream that there are
　　　　　　buzzards on the roof, or that a horse is stomping on you,
　　　　　　and the cat is on the roof. When a person has nightmares
　　　　　　like this, . . . [you know it is witchcraft]. Suppose that a
　　　　　　person had come to your house to ask to borrow something,
　　　　　　and then that night you dreamed that you are among a bunch
　　　　　　of people who want to kill you; then you *know* who it is
　　　　　　that is trying to bewitch you—the person to whom you re-
　　　　　　fused a favor.

However, only one "secure" identification was made through a dream, and this person was what will later be called a "core" witch. Normally, accounts reveal only that witchcraft is occurring.

Suspicious Encounters. Sometimes it is possible to attempt the identification of the witch by pinpointing the time and place of the witch's aggressive act, and then inferring the identity of the wrong-doer from the actions of those who were present. (This line of reasoning is facilitated by use of the third technique, motivational analysis, and is constrained by the length of time that has passed since the alleged encounter.) This method alone is an infrequent mode of identification. Out of the twenty-three cases that were sufficiently detailed, only one could be assigned to a suspicious encounter. An older woman who had been sick for three months had suspected witchcraft as the cause of her distress, had had the curer come and suck iron filings, thorns, meat, and *mescal* from her lower arm, and had reconstructed the identity of the aggressor by reference to an incident that had taken place just before the illness had begun. She told me after she had been cured: "I was standing in the little shop down the hill, when this man 'blew' in my direction. Now I realized that he was the one who was throwing those things into my body."

Motivational Analysis. Two major ways of reconstructing the motives for witchcraft exist. One can ask either of two questions: "With whom am I on such bad terms that he would want to bewitch me?" or "Who would stand to gain by my incapacitation or death?" Detective work is then required, because the person who stands to gain by one's injury is, in most cases, not the person who is doing the witchcraft. Most likely he or she has gone to another person (whose identity is not known) to ask him to use witchcraft powers on his or her behalf. For this reason the identity of the witch can only be speculative. If one has the nerve to confront his aggressor and demand that he divulge the identity of the witch, he would be making the wildest of accusations, and both the alleged aggressor and the purported witch would deny the accusation and accuse him of defamation. Thus, although a very large proportion of the recorded witchcraft incidents between living individuals could be typed as susceptible to motivational analysis, positive identification is rare and requires the cooperation of both the witch and the aggressor. For example, Evangelina is reported by some to be a witch (she appears in two of the six complete witch lists as Witch Number 14), and when she supposedly arranged that her husband's mistress be stricken with serious menstrual hemorrhaging, Amelia (who was the next-door neighbor and good friend of the mistress) could not be sure whether Evangelina had been the witch herself or had gotten someone else to do it for her. In most instances, the identity of the witch remains unknown, even though the aggressor can be identified.

CONCLUSION

The villager has a theory, or an explanation for witchcraft, just as the social scientist does. And they are not dissimilar. Where the social scientist looks for tension, the villager looks for envy. Where the social scientist examines interpersonal relations, the villager introspects about his relationships with other people. Where the social scientist looks for predisposing circumstances that will activate the process of a witch hunt, the villager looks at sickness and through diagnostics rationalizes the process of locating witches in the community. The social scientist admits the social definition of witches and accords them a reality that derives from cultural definition; the villager elaborates an ideology about the nature of the soul and its relationships with the animal and the spirit world. Both make the assumption that everyone agrees to the major propositions about the identification of witches (in this village through *tonos*) and the identity of witches. And in both cases they are deceiving themselves. It is not important that people do or do not agree on the criteria that define witches, or on who the witches are. The importance of witchcraft lies in the general process that generates witch identification and in the sociological consequences of the activity of labeling. Accordingly, I will now turn to an examination of that process.

6. Witchcraft and the Process of Labeling

In this chapter I shall leave the problem of the local ideology and turn to an account of the social process that I constructed in order to understand the criteria that the local people must have used to identify the witches they named. Once again I have recourse to the social model which I proposed in the earlier part of the book.

First, an axiom to which we must all agree is that there are no witches in the world. This sounds very obvious when read in the cold, rational hall of academe, but I myself have gotten confused on the matter. Certainly, I believe that there are people who can make others sick and even kill them by some mysterious, baleful psychological influence; we call such occurrences psychosomatic illnesses, for which we have a rather elaborate theory. It is equally clear that when I am working in the village I sometimes find it very difficult to believe that witches do not exist. One time, after I had been working solidly for two weeks and was running into difficulties with the data, Santos informed me in the course of a conversation that someone was gossiping about me and saying that I was a witch. I got very angry and hotly denied it and started into a long argument about my *tono*, about all the favors that I did, and so on. My wife happened to be present and suggested that maybe it was time for a break, and I caught myself and grinned foolishly. I then left for a long weekend. But when it comes right down to it, I will stake my reputation on the fact that no one has supernatural powers to sic his animal soul on me or to float mysterious, harmful objects through the air on his breath, insert them into my body, and sicken me, particularly when the objects are not microscopic, but visible objects, such as iron filings, thorns from cacti, *mescal*, and a wide range of household objects.

THE LABELING PROCESS

The structural argument that explains how concrete individuals are assigned to the category of "witch" can be summarized as follows: (1) Every person in the village believes in the existence of witches. (2) No one practices witchcraft or, equally, no one believes that he is a witch. (3) No two people believe that the witch group is made up of the same people; one's personal list of people who are witches is not shared with other people. (4) The greater the genealogical (kinship) and sociometric distance between informants, the lesser the degree of agreement about who the witches are, despite the existence of a "core" of agreement. Witch candidates are drawn by the villagers from the genealogically and sociometrically distant group of outsiders, and identification is validated by gossip about their activities.

Universality of Witches

Not one informant was found of about thirty interviewed or

contacted in suitable situations who did not believe in the existence
of witches. One young, progressive Protestant, who had been to
Mexico City to "study" with Pentecostal missionaries and who had
worked in the United States, had been repeatedly informed by his
theological mentors that Protestants had nothing to fear from
witchcraft because witches did not exist. Although he was an en-
thusiastic advocate of literacy, progressivism, and reform and in
general acted like a one-man Reformation, he was amused by the
credulity of his teachers in their mistaken notions that witchcraft
did not exist.

Absence of Self-Definition

It is virtually impossible to approach someone whom someone
else has accused of being a witch and ask him whether he concurs.
I did not know any putative witches well enough to put questions
like that to them in a sufficiently forceful way so as to elicit data
that I felt would be accurate. I also felt that it was unethical. Aside
from the fact that no one actually practices witchcraft, no one has
observed witchcraft, because by local definition it happens in a
hidden fashion; thus, there are no observable data to report. I do
know that the one person who is almost universally believed to be
a witch is unaware of his occult powers. Witch no. 1 (see Table 1)
is the most widely endorsed and universally excoriated witch in the
village. But when his wife ran away to Mexico City with another
man and he wished to practice witchcraft to bring her back, he went
to someone outside the village who *he* believed was a witch. The
outsider, a good friend of mine, is a rich peasant farmer and, like
most large land owners, has trouble acquiring a sufficient supply of
labor. He relies on his personal influence among the villagers in
this community and neighboring ones to attract the necessary field
hands to work for him. He encourages the belief that he is a witch
in order to make it difficult for people to refuse to work for him.
Witch no. 1 went to him and asked for help, and my friend asked

TABLE 1: WITCH LIST

			Informant's Name							
Witch No.	Sex	No. of Endorsements	Jesús	Santos	Amelia	Eusebia	Desideria	Jorge	Ángel I	Ángel II
1.	male	6	+	+	+	+	+		+	
2.	male	5	+	+	+		+	+		
3.	female	5	+	+	+	+			+	
4.	female	4	+		+	+				+
5.	male	4	+	+			+	+		
6.	female	3	+	+			+			
7.	male	3	+				+			+
8.	female	3	+	+				+		
9.	female	3			+			+		+
10.	male	3		+			+	+		
11.	male	2		+		+				
12.	female	2			+	+				
13.	female	2			+	+				
14.	female	2			+		+			
15.	female	1							+	
16.	male	1	+							
17.	female	1		+						
18.	male	1		+						
19.	female	1			+					
20.	male	1			+					
21.	female	1			+					
22.	female	1			+					
23.	female	1				+				
24.	male	1				+				
25.	male	1				+				
26.	male	1				+				
27.	female	1					+			
28.	female	1				+				
Total Witches Named			10	10	12	11	8	5	3	3

for a lock of his wife's hair, a black chicken, and a bottle of *mescal*. The wife returned within a fortnight but became seriously ill, and Witch no. 1 had to come again (another week's labor) to beg that the spell be taken off the wife because it had been too strong. The farmer was delighted with his magical ruse, the spell was lifted, the wife recovered, and she now lives with her "witch" husband in the village. The point is that the most virulent, the most danger-ous witch in the village, according to the villagers, is unaware of his power to do evil. (The farmer does not believe in witchcraft at all!)

Witch Groups

The data in the witch lists show that no two people think that the witch group is made up of the same people. I am not certain whether the informants are entirely aware of the discrepancies in the views of their society. Usually such care was taken to extract witch identifications that would not be contaminated by other people's opinions that informants were not confronted with the lack of agreement. But they certainly talked as though they believed that everyone agreed on who the witches were, and they often talked about them as though they were a visible, concrete group. This arose partly from the fact that curers are automatically sus-pected of having witch powers, and curers are visible. It also arises from the belief that *tonos* of the same kind stick together (as in the case of Merina's delinquent snake companions who "should have been there"), and, since there is no clear distinction between the person and the *tono*, one is forced to talk as though the actual people with the oversize cat *tonos* stuck together as well.

There is no consensus, as can be seen in the witch list. The results of my interviews with the eight informants who were sufficiently close to me to trust me with data on the identities of witches can be seen in the list. I conclude, then, that each member of the community has his own group of witches, which partially, but only partially, overlaps those of other members.

Witch Candidates

Candidates for one's group are drawn from those who are sociologically distant. I did not realize at first that everyone had his own list of witches. I thought, like most European-minded people (and quite a few anthropologists), that there was a sociologically definable group of people called "witches" in the community. Thus, after I had determined that witchcraft was an important form of deviance and that witches constituted an important category of deviant, I went looking for them. I had a good lead because the family I lived with pointed out that, although there were some witches around the house where I was living (Witch no. 1 lived two houses away, and Witch no. 10 was across the road and about twenty yards down the hill), most of the witches in the village did not live around our house—in the upper part of the village—but rather in the lower part. Fortunately, I had a very good informant who lived in the middle of the lower part, and I approached him carefully and discreetly in the hope that he would be of help in identifying the witches, whom I hoped subsequently to interview. He was. He pointed out that, although there were one or two witches in the lower part of the village, most of the witches lived in the upper part. Ironically enough, I still did not understand what they were saying, and I began to get very anxious that I would never get anywhere with the study because I would never be able to gain entry and establish rapport in the witch group.

Briefly, witches are drawn from the category of "those who live far away." An illness or sudden reversal of fortune initiates a search procedure among those who could have bewitched you in the way described in the last chapter. One operates from within his circle of kinsmen and reaches out through them to the rest of the village, attempting to impose his identification on others. The more one succeeds in this, the more of a witch the alleged assailant becomes. The identity of the witches depends upon one's position within the social structure and not at all on any intrinsic characteristic of the individual.

Let me demonstrate the proposition that definition depends on distance and that distance is defined by the social structure. First, I note that kinsmen are very important in the community and very sociologically close, and that no informant names a close consanguine kinsman in his witch list (i.e., closer than first cousin).

Another way of defining sociological closeness is to look at the layout of the village and its neighborhoods. Postmarital residential practices tend to gather patrilineally related kinsmen together. Subsequent neolocality (see Nutini, 1967, 1968, for discussion of residence practices in Middle America) does not create a marked degree of dispersion. Neighborhood interaction patterns have the same feel as was described in a more rigorous fashion by June Nash (1960, 1964) in her study of social relations in Amatenango del Valle in Chiapas. She noted that interaction rates rose with physical proximity and genealogical closeness. One interacts most frequently with kinsmen who are neighbors. Accordingly, I am going to assume that the greater the degree of physical removal from ego, the greater the tendency for any person to fall into the distant, unknown, unrelated category of persons from which ego draws his witches. By mapping the witches and the people who identify them over the village, then, I am going to expect to find that those witches whom, say, Santos, but no other informant, chose will be more distant from him than from the other informants. I will call them witch candidates and suggest that the process of labeling has begun for them. Witch no. 27 is a clear example. Eusebia picked her and utilized the general formula: "They say she is a witch," which can usually be translated to mean, "I think she is a witch"; but then she reflected and denied it, by stating, "But I don't believe it." No. 27's witch status is truly marginal in the sense that she is barely a witch candidate. We note that she lives a good distance from Eusebia but closer to the other informants, none of whom identify her as a witch. Another witch candidate is Witch no. 8, identified by Amelia. Jesús lives very close to this woman and does not name her; Jorge lives across the street and does not either. Desideria is as distant as Amelia, and we would hypothesize that she will be the next to join in the identification. We can extend this kind of statement to those witches who are picked by two people—they are endorsed by and large only by informants who are not kinsmen and who live far away from them.

At the other end of the scale we find that there are witches who are endorsed by six, five, four, or three people. These we can call the "core witches" in that there is a higher probability that an informant will include these people in his witch list. We can utilize the same logic that we used for the witch candidate and propose that if an informant identifies a neighbor as a witch, he will be a "core" witch, that is, there will be a high degree of consensus among our informants that the candidate is a witch. The maps of the village bear out these propositions. Map 1 shows an idealized representation of the demonstration of the hypothesis. As we move closer and closer to our informant (marked as X) we expect a progressively greater degree of endorsement. And, conversely, witch candidates are to be found on the periphery of the informant's social terrain.

Santos's choices show this dispersion best. Map 2 indicates where he lives, and the numbers indicate the number of endorsements from eight informants, as well as residences of the witches that he has named and the number of endorsements that each witch received. It is hypothesized that a person who is identified as a witch by Santos and who lives close to him will be widely endorsed. And, in general, the farther we go from Santos, the lesser the degree of endorsement. Relatively close to Santos's home we find that the

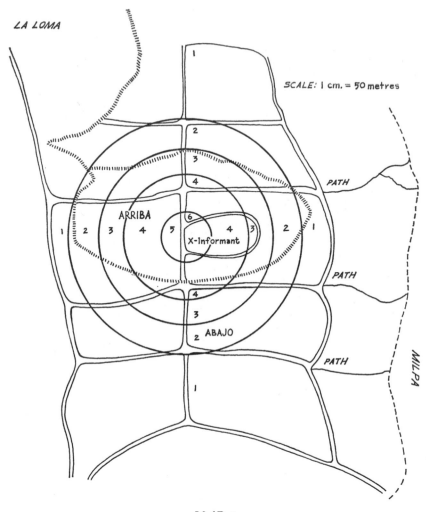

MAP 1

Ideal Representation of the Correlation between Distance and
Degree of Endorsement

Note:
(1) The closer the witch candidate is to the informant the greater the number
of endorsements by others before he will name him as a witch.
(2) The numbers refer to the number of endorsements required.

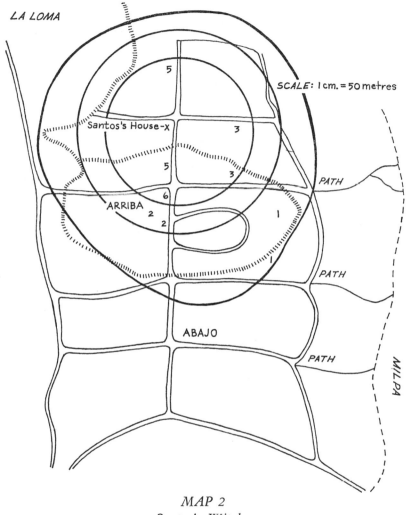

LA LOMA

SCALE: 1 cm. = 50 metres

Santos's House-x

ARRIBA

PATH

PATH

ABAJO

PATH

MILPA

5

3

5

3

6

2

2

1

1

MAP 2
Santos's Witches

Note: Numbers indicate place of residence and frequency of endorsement.

witches have received endorsements from three to six informants. Going progressively farther from his house, we find that the three next closest witches are endorsed by two informants. Outside these two concentric circles we find witches that only Santos names (one endorsement).

Map 3 shows the residences of all the witches named by the eight informants. The information coded in Map 3 indicates, through simple observation, that the hypothesis is correct. The villagers endorse the hypothesis as well. Amelia was describing an imaginary colloquy between two witches bent on doing harm, and she reported the following demoniacal protest at the suggestion that they stick close to home: "No, no, I am going to work a long way off, where there's nobody that's close to me." Then she added, parenthetically, "They do their harm to people who live away from them." Eusebia commented once on the misfortunes of a person who lives a good distance away from her: "They say that it's an illness of God, but how can we know, because, well, they are people who live well away from us." She also mentions that "everyone in [another village about five miles away] is a witch," indicating that people from a distant town who are unknown and who don't speak Zapotec clearly and properly constitute a population from which one draws witches. The majority of local witches who are not from the community come from the neighboring town, where the population is rife with witches.

How, then, does a person finally come to be labeled a witch? Quite simply, through the social process of gossip. In any social group, successful labeling of a deviant implies the success of moral entrepreneurs who are able to persuade the "good men" of the community that their labeling of deviants is valid. In the Zapotec village, the informants are quite explicit on the point that gossip serves to label people. Jorge points out that "whatever starts off as a gossipy tale lands up as the truth." Amelia agrees: "If there's something that happens to someone, people immediately start to

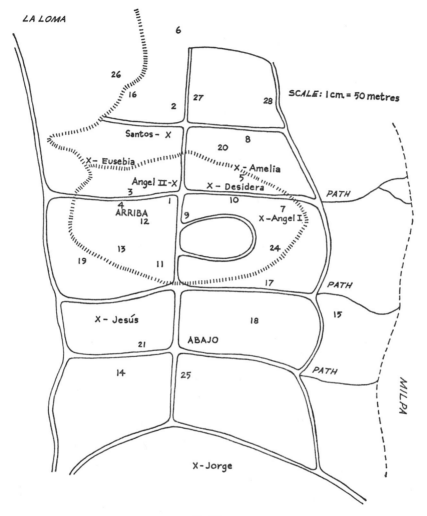

MAP 3
Locations of Witches and Informants

Note: This map has to be read in conjunction with the witch list, Table 1 in Chapter 6.

talk. The people decide what kind of an illness it is. They say that
it's a witchcraft illness, because so-and-so is trying to do her harm."
And the point is that "we cannot know the hearts of people who
are distant from us, and cannot have any way of checking out the
stories that we hear—so we believe them." Jesús points out that
there is a great difference between witch gossip and other kinds of
gossip; witch gossip is always true. That is, when witch stories
concern people that the villagers do not know at all well, they believe them and store the information away for future verification.
The resulting situation is very much like that which Fox (1967:
265) reports in Cochiti pueblo in the southwestern United States:
". . . practically everyone is suspected by someone at some time of
being a witch, or practicing sorcery."

Thus, it is that one draws his candidates from the distant and
unknowable populations and seeks validation for his choice through
gossip. Such information is encountered continually. Witch stories
are rife in the community—probably no other single kind of story
(with the exception of stories about illicit sex) arouses so much
interest. Progressive validation makes it possible for one to assign
to the witch category people who are progressively closer and closer
to one. A final decision that a neighbor or kinsman is a witch means
that the community as a whole has made the decision, and the
person is universally labeled a witch.

Once one has received a large number of endorsements, in particular from people who are close to him, his position in the village
becomes tenuous at best, and dangerous at worst. The person becomes isolated from everyone except those kinsmen who cannot
avoid him (his lineals).[1] His uncles and cousins and nephews simply avoid him entirely, or as much as they can without offending
him and bringing on an aggressive attack. He has to keep to himself or form ad hoc alliances with nonkin in order to survive. The

[1] This and the other implicit quantitative statement about kinship and interaction are doggedly documented in Selby (1966).

saint's day fiesta (*cuelga*) is a very important occasion for the rein-
forcement of ties, particularly with fictive kinsmen. Yet, no one
who is a "core witch" ever gives a saint's day party, probably because he knows that very few people would come—in particular
very few *kambali* (fictives), for whom the fiesta is given. Witch
no. 1, the most widely endorsed, is a pathetic figure in many ways.
Although he is very talkative, good humored, and traditional in
manner, no one will talk to him. He comes to *cuelgas*, and the interaction that takes place with him has the same quality of spurious-
ness that Lemert noted characterized "paranoids" and their associates. He peers out from behind the cactus fence at the passing scene,
pretending that he is working on a plough, all the while rather
desperate to talk to people. One is told to shield the children from
him and never to lend him money or speak with him if it can be
avoided. He has supposedly done terrible things in the village,
where his father was a witch before him. He has killed people,
maimed them, and done all manner of harm, or so it is reported.
To me, he looks like a tired, lonely old man who, despite his penu-
riousness, tries to save just enough to get drunk about once a month
and to feed his wife. He has no children. His eyes are failing now,
but when he was a younger man he used to read a lot. Now he
reads only his catechism. There were four men of his generation
who knew how to read. The others were all respected for their
wisdom and skill and were made president of the village; but not
he. He has never held political office. He grimly holds on in appall-
ing poverty, in the midst of hostility, in a world where he is an
odious scapegoat, and waits to die.

CONCLUSION

Clearly, the distinction between insiders and outsiders involves
a multitude of decisions about who is, or is not, going to be accused of being a witch. I reiterate that one does not go up to a
witch and accuse him to his face (as is reported to be done in some

other traditional communities); one reports one's discovery to the members of one's household (who have generally participated in the decision) and progressively communicates the information to members of one's inside group. It is also important to recall that the process of witch labeling goes on constantly; there are enough sudden deaths in this poor community to feed the process, and, in any case, the process is constantly being revised. It may take months or even years to produce a witch. Often the informants will report that "they never knew" that so-and-so was a witch, and therefore responsible for some serious illness of some years back, but now that such-and-such has happened the whole thing is clear. Witch identifications are constantly being mulled over, discussed, and revised within the inner circle.

Witch labeling is a sociological game, not just in the sense of assigning people to this deviant category, but in the sense that it is the dynamic form that interaction (and symbolic exchange) takes in defining the inner group, and thereby the outsiders. Amelia is a delightful informant because she is so ingenuous, and what appear to be inconsistencies in her statements usually contain a goodly portion of truth. We were talking about someone who is widely reputed to be a witch, and she said, "I know that people say she's a witch, but I don't believe it, because I go and ask her for things— like a bit of corn or some firewood—and she always does me the favor." Amelia is not aware of the explanation I have been developing here, but she is aware that, if one engages in symbolic exchange with someone, that person is a member of the inner group and therefore cannot be described as a witch.

I have insisted throughout this account that symbolic exchange is the major activity that creates community, and I pointed out that the local ideas about "good" could be summarized as the necessary conditions for acceptable exchange relationships on three levels— the individual ("trust"), the interpersonal ("humility"), and the sociological ("respect"). I have tried to explain how deviance, values, and society are all the same thing in the sense that each serves to define the other, and to talk about one is to talk about the others. That was the reason I devoted so much time to kinship. The kinship model is the model for good and for evil, and the implications of this kinship model are worked out sometimes in conscious, and at other times in unconscious, ways so that the social order is a moral order, and society and deviance are the same.

Why, then, do human beings not realize this? Why are they forever creating explanations for their conduct that are ad hoc and epiphenomenal and do not reflect, but rather conceal, the sociological imperatives to which they are responding? This, finally, is where psychology comes in; two aspects of human psychology bear on the answer to this question. The first is less familiar to most readers because it lies in what we can call human nature. Lévi-Strauss (cf., for example, 1962) has devoted twenty years of his life to examining the way in which human beings play with ideas and use society to think with, as well as to live in. Society is one of man's most productive ideas, as well as most distinctive inventions, and it is man's nature to be creative, imaginative, and fanciful with his own creations in a way that the French anthropologist has described so allusively and powerfully. Social anthropologists have rejected the older definitions of man, such as man the toolmaker (*Homo faber*), and replaced them with a definition of man the classifying animal (*Homo taxonomicus*). Society, in French, is *bonne à penser*, something that man can use to fashion his myths and his art, his ideologies and his cosmologies. We were viewing a tiny sample of that creativity when I described the Zapotec explanations for witchcraft.

But psychology, in the more usual sense, is also important in understanding why we make up myths about deviance, since we presumably do so in response to both anxieties and conflicts, as well as conscious needs and ambitions. It is psychologically important to believe what we believe about sin, just as it is psychologically important for the Zapotecs to believe in souls and incest. There is a psychology of deviance in Zapotec, and even more so in Western thought, but I contend that the essence of understanding deviance lies not here, but in an understanding of the social reality that generates deviance in ways that the Zapotecs are more cognizant of than we are, but that even escape their extensive capacity for abstract and sociological thought.

7. The Origins of Good and Evil

One last accounting needs to be made, and that is a rendering of the origins of good and evil. So far I have talked a great deal about the relationship between good, evil, and society, but it has been a disembodied account in the sense that any synchronic, structural account must be.

I would like to conclude the discussion by sketching out some ideas about the determinants of the value system. If deviance and values are in a close relationship, then to explain one in terms of the other, as I have done here, is tautologous. We have to get out of this circular argument somehow to explain where the values came from, if the explanation is to be at all adequate. This is the kind of intellectual venture that Marxist writers have handled very well, and, although I am not myself a Marxist, I do think that the problem of tautology should be acknowledged and dealt with.

I can put the problem as follows, in the language of this case study: why did the villagers choose "humility," "trust," and "respect," and why not "self-reliance," "inner peace," and "ambition," or some other dimensions? Two kinds of explanation can be used to explain the particular configuration of values of a community: an explanation based on the adaptive potential of a particular set of values or a historical explanation, which shows how such values developed over time. I avoid the first because it is logically impossible to handle, unless one is willing to treat all other possible value configurations and devise some criterion of adaptive potential that will enable one to decide which is the most adaptive. In addition, I would find it difficult to make the argument that the value system of the village had a high degree of adaptive potential, if we agree that adaptation refers to the process whereby an individual or collectivity extracts some maximum benefit from its ecological niche and maintains a living system in some kind of dynamic equilibrium. In a world where competition for scarce capital and resources is increasingly important, the value system of the village prohibits the efficient use of the resources it has and impedes the exploitation of resources outside the community. One would have trouble attempting to justify humility, trust, and respect as bases for operating in a mixed economy where maximization is the norm. It would be much easier to make the argument that village values are maladaptive because they have contributed to the marginality of the economic and ecological position of the village. The emphasis on humility, on quiescence, and on the maintenance of internal harmony has permitted the manipulation, exploitation, and oppression of the villagers and has ruled out an effective response to outside pressures emanating from government or capitalist entrepreneurs. In short, I do not believe that these values are adaptive in the present world.

A historical explanation is more interesting and more useful. This Zapotec village is an instance of a type of community called a "closed corporate community." First, it is "corporate" because a major resource (common land) is held, not in the name of individuals, but in the name of the community as a whole. The village-corporation has an "estate," in the old-fashioned legal terminology. Second, it is a corporation because it can act as a single individual, and, viewed from the outside, it can be seen as a single individual. Its officers act in the name of the corporation when they deal with the outside world. Third, it has an internal organization independent of the particular members of the corporation: president, secretary, *mayordomo* of the patron saint, and so on, and the organization of these offices constitutes a corporate structure. It also has the power to tax itself and the power to carry out judicial proceedings in its own name (subject to review in the case of major criminal acts). It is "closed" because the membership is co-opted from within. Endogamous marriage practices assure that both parents of all children in the corporation will be community members. In the 1965 census, over 90 percent of the marriages in the community were endogamous. That figure is much higher for first marriages and is not overly high for traditional communities in Mesoamerica. It is difficult for people to immigrate into the community unless they have some close kinship ties with the community, and in any case they have to wait a generation until they have clear rights of usufruct on common lands.

Further, it is a *community* because the village is the major source of identity for the members of the corporation. Demeteria was very confused about us for a long time, because we identified ourselves as Americans, and therefore she felt that we must be members of a village called America. We returned one year to find her very worried because she had heard that America was at war with another community, Vietnam, and she was afraid that we and our families would be killed. To her way of thinking, a war is a feud between two neighboring villages: the idea that our community was at war with another community ten thousand miles away was incomprehensible. She is aware of the existence of national states; she has been to Mexico City and her son works there, but we had identified ourselves as Americans, and therefore our village must go by that name, because people identify themselves by using the name of their village. As far as the outside world is concerned, one is first a community member.

There does not seem to be any reason to believe that this has not been true from the precolonial period. One of the striking things about the history of the Oaxaca Valley, in contrast to northern Mexico and the central highlands, is the continuity of traditions from the early period. The Conquest was not nearly so traumatic in Oaxaca as it was in the north. Whereas those in the Aztec capital suffered a bloody carnage and wholesale assault upon their religion and their state, the Spaniards played the role of benefactor to the Zapotec. Their landing served to raise the siege at Tehuantepec and saved the Zapotec capital from the hands of the Aztecs, who had to hasten north to meet the new threat from the sea. The Spanish occupation of the valley was welcomed since it relieved the pressure on the Zapotec nation from the increasing hegemony of the Mixtecs. The *marquesado* of the valley was an immense domain, and the *marqués*, Cortez himself, preferred the method of indirect rule. Better the loyal Zapotec nobility than scheming and predatory Spaniards. And unlike what happened in the central highlands, the nobility was not systematically exterminated or dispossessed, nor were Spanish masters set up to replace the local Zapotec lords.

Following the Conquest, depopulation took place followed by an economic depression that was linked both to the depletion of population and to a depression in Europe. But the answer that was devised to these threats to the living styles and standards of the ruling class—the *hacienda*—never really took root in Oaxaca in the way that has been described for so much of Mexico. (See for example Wolf's 1955, 1957, and 1959 discussions of the *hacienda* and its place in the development of the closed corporate community, as well as Chevalier's 1952, 1960, and 1963 discussions.)

There were certainly economic effects from the Conquest. Domestic animals were introduced, and with the growth of a mining industry to the southwest the demand for hides, tallow, and meat offered great incentives to the Spanish rancher to expand his holdings at the expense of the Indian and to convert farming land into pasture. But the Indian was not slow to defend his rights through litigation, and the lands in the branch of the valley where the community is situated were so needed to grow wheat that was necessary to feed the growing capital of Antequera that the cattle men never made serious inroads on the Indian wheat and corn farming land (Taylor, 1972:120). To be sure, the viceroy encouraged the Spanish ownership of wheat-growing land, but rather than encroach on Indian lands, swamps were drained and allotted to Spaniards.

Because of Wolf's work on corporate communities it has become routine wisdom to regard their growth as an outcome of the imposition of the *hacienda* system. It is true that during the seventeenth century *haciendas* were established in the general area of the community, but it is also true that, despite the great value of the land in the area, these *haciendas* never developed the techniques of exploitation, debt peonage, territorial expansion, and totalitarianism that are associated with the development of that institution in the north of Mexico. For one thing, it was rare that the *hacienda* was in stable ownership. The history of Oaxaca in the colonial period is a history of bankruptcies (particularly during the depression years of the early eighteenth century), sales, and alienations in the absence of a stable landed gentry. Almost without exception estates were mortgaged to the hilt, and were only marginal economic successes. Second, entailment was comparatively rare. This meant that there was no legal barrier to the sale or alienation of property. Third, the practice of ecclesiastical *mortmain*, or the legal right to all property *ever* owned by the Church, was not maintained in the valley. And last, the Indians were never slow to defend themselves and their communities from the encroachments of the *hacen-*

dados. They were litigious and effective. They were able to extract
more advantage from the *hacendado* than in the north, as the debt
records and the constant complaints about labor shortages attest.[1]
Where the Church aggrandized its property holdings, as it did during the eighteenth century, it did so at the expense of the Spanish
landholders, and not at the expense of the Indians. Taylor (1972:
201) concludes that the only stable holdings in the valley during
the eighteenth century were the Indian holdings, and that Indians
controlled about two-thirds of the land during the final century of
the colonial period.

Thus, the picture of oppression, exploitation, and disinheritance
that caused Wolf (1959:213) to call this period an "open wound
on the body of Middle American society that has endured to this
day" simply did not occur in the Oaxaca Valley, and particularly in
that part of the valley where the community is. And the results can
be seen even today. There is an absence of invidious "racial" distinctions between Indian and mestizo, as between townsman and
villager. A colleague of mine who carried out extensive work in
Guatemala once remarked that there were no Indians in the valley
of Oaxaca, and his middle-class-townsman interlocutor, reflecting
the view of the city, replied, "We are *all* Indians." The Revolution
did not affect the valley of Oaxaca very greatly. The ringing cry for
"bread and land" was hardly calculated to resonate in the breasts of
those who had them already. Today both peasant and Indian seem
inclined to deny the propaganda of their educators and regard the
hacienda period as a kind of golden age. They talk about stable
prices and wages; the easy acquisition of livestock; the "hard, big"
peso, which could buy one hundred tortillas (versus eight today);
the availability of work and help in necessity. Even allowing for
nostalgic euphoria, the investigator would be hard-pressed to sus-
tain the thesis that the colonial and revolutionary periods were ones
of sustained oppression.

[1] This material is drawn from Taylor (1972), which I have used extensively
in this section.

I cite all this historical data to make a simple point: there was continuity in social and cultural tradition from the precolonial period through the colonial period extending into the revolutionary period and even into the time of the Second World War. The closed corporate community that we observe today in the valley is not a disfigured mockery of the indigenous organization, but a present-day evolutionary product, a transformation of a tradition that antedates the Conquest. The question then concerns the connection between the ecological and political realm and the domain of values: humility, trust, and respect. My argument is that two central institutional focuses organize social relations in these communities, and that they are premised on the adherence to the three value conceptions as I have outlined them earlier. The two institutions are (1) the civil-religious hierarchy and (2) the organization of interpersonal relations through the medium and ideology of kinship.

The civil-religious hierarchy in Middle America predates the Conquest and can be seen not only as a means to structure political roles in the community but also as an effective leveling device that keeps all members of the community at about the same economic level, thus maintaining the premise of equality. In this political system the sacred offices and the political offices are interlinked. As a young married man, the villager starts at the bottom of the ladder and works his way up in the prestige system of the village by successively holding civil and religious posts, until he becomes a respected elder, or *principal*, in his old age. He gains prestige by the lavish expenditure of wealth in fulfillment of his sacred or secular posts. Every saint has a sponsor, or *mayordomo*, and a festival. Celebration of the festival requires the expenditure of a great amount of money, and the sponsor may pay for the mass, the music, the fireworks, the food, and the drink, as well as all the sacred trappings of the saints. Since each festival is village wide, one must provide a good deal. Augustino, who was *mayordomo del santito patrón*, reckoned that he spent upward of five thousand pesos (in present-day values) and his major capital resource (four head of cattle) on his office as well as going so deeply into debt as to require four years to pay off his *compadres* and relatives. There is no reason to believe that expenses were proportionately smaller in earlier times, and one can easily see that the civil-religious hierarchy can act to bring individuals down to a general level of subsistence if they are fortunate enough to get ahead financially and acquire some small amount of capital. The civil-religious hierarchy operated so as to convert material goods into prestige and at the same time keep individuals from rising out of the general level of poverty that burdened all of them. If one rose in the world, it was in terms of prestige, and as far as we know people who would not conform were subject, just as they are today, to attacks of *envidia* and witchcraft that left their lives and fortunes in great jeopardy.

The civil-religious hierarchy and the associated value system have proved very durable. Fully developed systems still exist in the Oaxaca Valley and elsewhere in Mesoamerica despite the urgent efforts of the government to eliminate them and thereby aid the peasant farmer in the process of capital formation.

The second component of community social organization is kinship. It also operates as a leveling mechanism in these communities, as it does in all communities where there are no institutionalized arrangements to create castes, or hierarchies, based on stratified orderings of kinship terms.[2] In general, the only way kinship can be

[2] This is a statement that would require at least a book in itself to justify. The anthropological literature on kinship is very extensive, as can be seen by looking at a recent recension carried out by Buchler and Selby (1968). In general, it can be summarized in the following way: Although kinship categories can be used to reflect status differences between members of society, this can only take place where there are marriage rules that encode status differences between intermarrying groups and forbid marriages that would confound prevailing orderings. South India provides a good instance of these systems of marriage— here, a person is born into a descent group that is recruited on the basis of patriliny. It is a well-defined group, so that no one is a member of two groups and every person is a member of one, and only one, group of patrilineally related

used to encode status differentials is to recruit *well-defined* groups
on the basis of kinship. This implies that there is a community rule
that associates every member to one, and only one, group, and that
the groups are rank ordered. Usually (see footnote 2) the ranking
criterion is associated with marriage, and there is a complex marriage rule, framed in the idiom of kinship, that keeps marriages
and status classes in order. Well-defined groups are absent in this
community, as they are in most (but not all) of Mesoamerica. The
village kinship system, as I pointed out, is not unlike ours. Villagers trace relationship through both men and women, and every person is a member of a number of overlapping kindreds; there is no
distinct borderline between groups. An example from our own society can illustrate what I mean by overlapping kindreds and indis-
tinct groups. I may be invited to Thanksgiving dinner by two first
cousins on different sides of my family. I am a member of the kinship group of both, although they may feel that they belong to different kindreds. I cannot decide which dinner to attend on the
basis of my membership in a kinship group, because I am equally
a member of both of my cousins' kindreds. There is no way I can
use the idiom of kinship to form discrete, well-defined groups. Of
course there may be inequalities of status between two members of
a kindred. I am told that when the very extensive Romney kindred

kinsmen. The marriage rule encodes the cultural fact that one marries a woman
of inferior status. When one marries, one creates a status relationship between
two groups: his patrilineal group is superior to her patrilineal group by virtue
of the fact that he married her. His sister cannot marry a man of that group, because his group would be simultaneously inferior and superior to the same
group, and status relations would be impossible to manage. The rule of marriage
must cover this contingency and create classes of marriageable people so that both
men and women marry consistently within the status rules (and of course the
exogamous prescriptions). This is often carried out by framing the rules in the
idiom of kinship, and kinship serves to encode inequality or differences in status
(see Lévi-Strauss [1949] and Leach [1954] for elaborate discussions of systems
like this). Well-defined descent groups, status differences, and explicit marriage
rules that keep the marriage classes straight do not exist in Mesoamerica.

gathers, among the 750 first cousins of George Romney, he is generally granted a higher status, but it is not accorded to him by virtue of his kinship relationship.

There are relative differences in status between my kin and myself, but these are reciprocal. Uncles are superior to me, to be sure,
but I myself am nephew to some but uncle to others, father-in-law
to some, and son-in-law to others. There is no way I can derive an
absolute status difference between myself and some other class of
people, based on kinship. In this kind of community, the degree to
which kinship encodes the ideology of social intercourse marks the
degree to which symmetry and amity, exchange and reciprocity
characterize (ideally) interpersonal relations. (Conversely, the degree to which we are status conscious marks the degree to which
we have departed from the idiom of kinship as a means of express-
ing our social relationships.) Fortes (1969) has discussed what
he calls the "axiom of amity" in kinship relations. He adduces a
multitude of ethnographic statements and ethnographer's com-
ments to show that, however the kinship domain is defined, relations among kinsmen are morally premised on generosity, amity,
and a sense of justice. He cites a passage of Oliver's (1955:454–
455) as a concise statement of what his lifetime study of the premises of kinship relations worldwide has led him to believe:

Mankind consists of relatives and strangers. Relatives are usually interlinked by both blood and marital ties; most of them live nearby, and
persons who live nearby are all relatives. Relatives should interact quite
frequently and at least in times of crises and on the occasion of one another's rites of passage. Transactions among them should be carried out
devoid of a spirit of commerciality—preferably consisting of sharing,
nonreciprocable giving, and bequeathing, among closest relatives, or of
lending, among more distantly related ones. Among themselves relatives
should feel and express emotions of affection, or at least amity—colored,
when appropriate, by expressions of deference, or polite constraint, and
of sex avoidance.

I think that the villagers I have been describing would endorse that statement, however much they might shake their heads at the idealistic tone. But when they talk about their misgivings and about their slights, it seems clear to me that they do accede to this premise about the quality of social relations of kinship.

I witnessed a dramatic instance of the restraining power of kinship in 1965. I was interviewing a friend when a drunken man staggered into the room carrying a bottle. He was greeted and asked to sit down, which he did, almost falling off the low stool. He brandished the bottle and we drank together, even though he clearly was already drunk. Suddenly, he fished into his loose white cotton trousers, hauled out a pistol, and began to wave it around the room. I was terrified but determined not to show it, and we drank again while our companion expatiated on the virtues of his weapon. He lurched to his feet and staggered into the patio where a little girl was playing. He didn't see her but pointed the pistol in her general direction and cocked the weapon. At that point I grabbed him and hauled him back into the house; we sat down and drank again. During this episode, neither my friend nor his wife, to whom the child had run for comfort, showed the slightest resentment of his behavior. After about fifteen minutes he left, cordially escorted from the house by his host. When the latter came back, I couldn't restrain myself, and I asked him why on earth he had not stopped the stranger from brandishing his pistol and menacing the life of his child. The reply was simple: "How could I? He was my brother-in-law!" Any action on the part of our host that would have contravened the axiom of amity or served to impute distrust or disrespect would have been ungenerous and would have run against his deeply felt conviction about the nature of kinship relations.

The value system, then, and the associated beliefs about deviant conduct are a residue of a history that reaches back centuries to the time of the Conquest. The civil-religious hierarchy and the deeply felt and enduring structure of kinship relations were combined with the *hacienda* system to produce a social order both internal and external to the community, which acted to enshrine and perpetuate the values of humility, trust, and respect. But the village is changing now. These values that have maintained an isolated democracy have become maladaptive in an increasingly individualized and commercialized world. Perhaps this system will not last out the century. More and more villagers are voting against the system with their feet: leaving for the city. Both those who stay and those who go are aware now, as always, that they live in a stratified society and that they are at the bottom of the heap. They know well that when the benefits of the society are passed out, they are the last to receive, and then in small measure. They know that there is too much sickness now, as before, even though things may be better than they were in the past. They know that they work too hard for too little. Still they look to the future with hope, in the assurance that things will materially improve for them. They see evidence of improvement all around them. In the last five years they have built a new school (with some help from local, state, and national sources) and an irrigation system. The roads are improved; electricity and even television have arrived. Jesús believes that these are all surface changes, ameliorations of a bitter life, and all to the good. Jesús says that villages will always be and that the life he leads today will be unchanged in any deep way until the day he dies. The village has survived the Conquest, the *hacienda*, the Revolution, and modern bureaucracy, and it has retained a profound feeling of self-respect and identity. One hopes that in Mexico, as in the United States and elsewhere, it will be possible to create a social system in which people will neither be deprived of their share of the nation's resources nor be culturally subverted in the name of conformity, efficiency, and rationality.

APPENDIX

Mean Rank Order of Deviance Items (from Bad to Good)

Rank Order	Mean Ranking	Short Gloss	Item Number
1	2.6	Murderer	27
2	6.8	Abortionist	34
3	7.2	Robber	40
4	8.9	Knows witchcraft	15
5	10.0	Supernatural gossip	4
6	10.2	Performs witchcraft	11
7	12.6	Witch	38
8	14.7	Fights with neighbor	41
9	15.3	Delicate	37
10	15.5	Frightens children	10
11	15.9	Evil gossip	26
12	16.3	Uninterpretable item	36
13	16.4	Contemptuous person	16
14	18.3	Evil manner	5
15	18.6	Aggressive and bad-tempered	28
16	19.2	Nosey person	32
17	19.4	"Judger"	8
18	20.7	Ungenerous	1
19	20.8	Lazy and vice-ridden	21
20	21.7	Fighter (woman)	45
21	21.7	Unbeliever	7
22	21.9	Outspoken	35
23	22.2	Abandons child (woman)	9
24	23.2	Liar	20
25	24.9	Adulteress	30
26	25.3	Stingy person	6
27	25.4	Envious person	25
28	26.7	Poor drinker	23
29	27.1	Evil eye	31
30	27.9	Abandons nursing mother	14
31	28.2	Proud of self	39
32	28.5	Busybody	33
33	29.1	Adulterer	17
34	30.1	Shameless person	43
35	30.9	Angry person	22
36	31.1	Lazy	29
37	31.2	Quiet (silent person)	24
38	31.8	Untrusting person	2
39	33.5	A "hard" person	19
40	34.9	Drunkard	46
41	35.6	Lecher	3
42	36.3	Homosexual	44
43	36.4	Has familiar-spirit power	42
44	41.8	Helps neighbor	12
45	42.4	Unsuitable item	13
46	42.4	Does favors	18

The Deviance Items

Item	Ordinal Rank	Mean Rank	Zapotec	Spanish	English
1	18	20.7	njó'tin 'unin favor	no sabe hacer favor	doesn't know how to do favors
2	38	31.8	ráka šíntí làačin	el es desconfiado	an untrusting person
3	41	35.6	čínti náda kamó'ten, nuní' nen kabiñ kúnni	también el tiene el vicio de hablar con las muchachas	the lecher
4	5	10.1	wana biéha	buena vieja	supernatural gossip
5	14	18.3	túšu čaab na' mo'ten	el tiene modo muy feo	has an evil way about him
6	26	25.3	rná'tin 'ákane 'átin biní	no le gusta prestar a otra persona	doesn't like to lend to others
7	20	21.7	ne tub kósa rčéet làacin	ni una cosa no se cree	the unbeliever
8	17	19.4	ruíakan kapsíntin	juzga a su vecino	judges his neighbor
9	23	22.2	rsanján ka'ši'nin	abandona a sus hijos	she abandons her children
10	10	15.5	ne kamdomá'tin rčíbkan tanto čaab na mo'ten	también se asustan sus criaturas tan feo es su modo	even his children are frightened of him, his character is so ugly
11	6	10.2	baaštin kosa mal tí'ši biní'	tiró en el cuerpo de ella	he threw some harmful substance in her body
12	44	41.8	ra nu ró'o' run kapsíntin	cualquier cosa se le da a su vecino	will always help out a neighbor
13	---	---	Unsuitable item		
14	30	27.9	ríut la'čínne' žal kaane' mdo'	a el no le gusta la mujer porque está criando	he doesn't enjoy women when they are nursing a child
15	4	8.9	ní'tušu njú'bin 'únin daño te' lo' sa'an	esa persona sabe hacer much daño a su compañero	this person knows how to do a lot of harm to his fellow man (through witchcraft)
16	13	16.4	ršti'n lo šínim bauían biní'	el tira su saliva de ver una persona	he spits when he sees someone

Item	Ordinal Rank	Mean Rank	Zapotec	Spanish	English
17	33	29.1	ka štú'n	tiene su querida	is an adulterer
18	46	42.4	kwalker šíni' rúnin favor	cualquier cosa el hace el favor	will do any kind of favor
19	39	33.5	tušu dí'tan	es muy duro	a "hard" man
20	24	23.2	ni' ríu'laačin únlaačin	a el le gusta decir mentiras	likes to tell lies
21	19	20.8	riáltin no 'oon nu že'n pur ka visju tíni, ríča laáčin	el no busca de comer, no más anda con sus vicios	he doesn't try to make his way, merely indulges his vices
22	35	30.9	rún šiánten	está enojado	is habitually angry
23	28	26.7	lo' či' no'kan re'kan loy rni'n	cuando algunos estan tomando, el habla mal de ellos	when people are drinking together he speaks evil of them
24	37	31.2	ni'i rnàatin nin	el no quiere hablar	he doesn't want to talk
25	27	25.4	ni'i tušu ráka nálaačin te kamjeti	esa persona tiene envidia de la gente	this person has envy of others
26	11	15.9	rni'i ča'ban te kamjeti	habla mal de las gentes	speaks evil of others
27	1	2.62	rú'tin lo' sa'n	mata a sus compañeros	kills his fellow villagers
28	15	18.6	neka bailo'tukan 'u'tin kabini rle'tin	parece que no más con sus ojos puede matar a otra persona	appears that he can kill people with his eyes alone
29	36	31.1	ni'i nelódi tu' čin re'tin	ni tan siquiera ni a un trabajo va el	doesn't do any work at all
30	25	24.9	bí'ni ka' štu'n	ella tiene su querido	she has a lover
31	29	27.1	tušu lo'n	tiene mala cara	has an evil face (i.e., gives off the evil eye)
32	16	19.2	rči'žir de'nin ka kosa te' kamjeti	registra las cosas de la gente	is very nosey with other people's property
33	32	28.5	ni'i ríulaačin aka' tu' lo'n ne ni'i	a el le gusta mucho parejar con las gentes sin saberlo	he likes to make himself the equal of others without the ability ("butts in")

Item	Ordinal Rank	Mean Rank	Zapotec	Spanish	English
34	2	6.8	bi'ní bí'tin ši'nin lobžínin nó'tin	mató a la criatura cuando sentía que lo tenía	performed an abortion on herself
35	22	21.9	ne lo tub kosa rčí'btin rín	ni una cosa no se asusta decirlo	is not afraid to say anything
36	....	.....	uninterpretable item		
37	9	15.3	nelodi 'aka'že ka'mdoma' le'žatin	ni tan siquiera pueden ir las criaturas en el patio de el	little children cannot even go into his patio
38	7	12.6	biní nan brujo	esa persona es brujo	this person is a witch
39	31	28.2	rún rúban ruí'an žu'bin	se cree grande de verse de sí mismo	is very proud of himself
40	3	7.2	rba'nan te' sa'an	roba a su compañero	robs his fellow villager
41	8	14.7	kada ratu rtílan nen psíntin	cada rato pelea con su vecino	every little while he fights with his neighbor
42	43	36.4	ní'i rnà'a laàcin	el tiene su tono	has supernatural power from his familiar spirit
43	34	30.1	nu' biú' rtud ló'ni	es hombre sin vergüenza	is a person without shame
44	42	36.3	biní nan braš	el es manflor	is a homosexual
45	20	21.7	tusu rtí'lan	ella pelea mucho	she fights a great deal
46	40	34.9	tusu re'n	toma mucho	drinks a good deal

A Componential Account of Kinship Categories of Reference

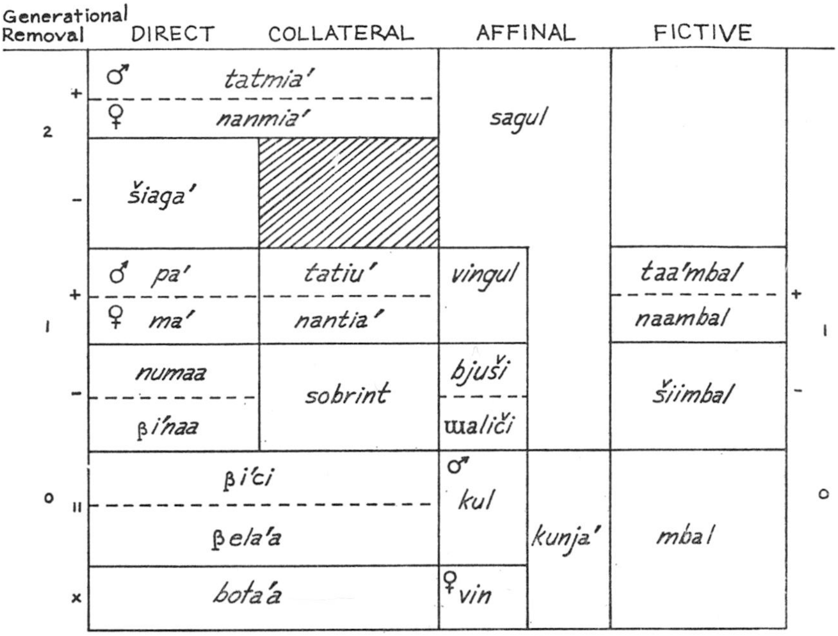
Generational Removal
DIRECT
COLLATERAL
AFFINAL
FICTIVE
+
2
-
+
1
-
0
II
x
♂ tatmia'
♀ nanmia'
sagul
šiaga'
♂ pa'
♀ ma'
tatiu'
nantia'
vingul
taa'mbal
naambal
numaa
βi'naa
sobrint
bjuši
ɯaliči
šiimbal
βi'ci
βela'a
♂ kul
kunja'
mbal
bota'a
♀ vin

Notes:

[1] The componential model was derived according to the Romney (1965) algorithm. For discussion of the problems and advantages to componential analysis, see Buchler and Selby (1968). These data are given for the anthropologists.

[2] Dotted lines indicate sex difference within the box. Males are in the upper part of the box, and females on the lower. Where there is no dotted line, no sex distinction is made.

[3] Some good Spanish speakers did not extend the sibling terms for cousins but used the Spanish terms *primo* and *prima*. Some people reported a fourth-degree affinal term, *kunja' prim*, which meant a distant affine. Usage was inconsistent.

[4] The cross-hatched area indicates the absence of kinship definition. People who occupy this space are "nothing to me."

[5] This analysis hypothesizes a six-dimensional space for referential kinship categories in this community. The components would be (1) sex of relative (male, female); (2) absolute generation (number of generations removed from ego, zero, one, two); (3) polarity (plus, minus); (4) sex of speaker (male, female; but applies only to zero generation, direct, and collateral); (5) direct/collateral; and (6) respect relation (which would distinguish affines and fictives from the rest of the data and would group them separately according to whether they were a category of marriage or a category of *compadrazgo*).

BIBLIOGRAPHY

Adams, R. N., and Arthur J. Rubel
  1967. "Sickness and Social Relations." In *Handbook of Middle American Indians*, edited by R. Wauchope, VI, 333–356. Austin: University of Texas Press.
Allport, Floyd H., and Leo J. Postman
  1945. "Wartime Rumors of Waste and Special Privilege." *Transactions of New York Academy of Science* 8:61–81.
  1946. "An Analysis of Rumor." *Public Opinion Quarterly* 10:501–517.
  1947. *The Psychology of Rumor.* New York: Holt, Rinehart and Winston.
Basso, Keith H.
  1966. *The Gift of Changing Woman.* Bulletin of the Bureau of American Ethnology, no. 196. Washington, D.C.: Smithsonian Institution.
  1969. *Western Apache Witchcraft.* Anthropological Papers of the University of Arizona, no. 15. Tucson: University of Arizona Press.
Beattie, John
  1963. "Sorcery in Bunyoro." In *Witchcraft and Sorcery in East Africa*, edited by John Middleton and Edward Winter. London: Routledge and Kegan Paul.
Becker, Howard S.
  1963. *Outsiders: Studies in the Sociology of Deviance.* New York: Free Press.

1964. *The Other Side: Perspectives on Deviance.* New York: Free Press.

1973. "Labelling Theory Revisited." In *Outsiders,* by Howard S. Becker, 12th Printing. New York: Free Press.

Berndt, Ronald M.

1958. "A Devastating Disease Syndrome: Kuru Sorcery in the Eastern Central Highlands of New Guinea." *Sociologus* 8:68–82.

Boas, Franz

1930. *The Religion of the Kwakiutl.* New York: Columbia University Press.

Bohannon, Paul

1958. "Extra-Processual Events in Tiv Political Institutions." *American Anthropologist* 60:1–12.

Buchler, I. R., and H. A. Selby

1968. *Kinship and Social Organization.* New York: Macmillan.

Bunzel, R.

1952. *Chichicastenango: A Guatemalan Indian Village.* Publication of the American Ethnological Society, no. 22. Locust Valley, N.J.: J. J. Augustin.

Cameron, N.

1943. "The Paranoid Pseudocommunity." *American Journal of Sociology* 46:33–38.

1959. "The Paranoid Pseudocommunity Revisited." *American Journal of Sociology* 65:52–58.

Chevalier, François

1952. *La formation des grandes domaines au Mexique: Terre et société aux XVIᵉ–XVIIᵉ siècles.* Paris.

1960. "Le grand domaine au Mexique du XVIᵉ au début de XIXᵉ siècle." In *Contributions à la Première Conférence Internationale d'Histoire Economique,* pp. 399–407. Stockholm.

1963. "The North Mexican Hacienda." In *The New World Looks at Its History,* edited by Archibald R. Lewis and Thomas F. McGann, pp. 95–107. Austin: University of Texas Press.

Cordry, Donald, and Dorothy Cordry

1968. *Mexican Indian Costumes.* Austin: University of Texas Press.

Court-Brown, W. M., and P. G. Smith
  1969. "Human Population Cytogenetics." *British Medical Bulletin* 25:74–80.
Dalton, Melville
  1959. *Men Who Manage.* New York: Wiley.
Douglas, Jack D.
  1970. *Deviance and Respectability.* New York: Basic Books.
Douglas, Mary
  1963. "Techniques of Sorcery Control in Central Africa." In *Witchcraft and Sorcery in East Africa*, edited by John Middleton and Edward Winter. London: Routledge and Kegan Paul.
El Guindi, Fadwa
  1971. "The Nature of Belief Systems: A Structural Analysis in a Zapotec Community." Paper presented at the American Anthropological Association, 1971.
  1972. "The Nature of Belief Systems: A Structural Analysis of Zapotec Ritual." Ph.D. dissertation, University of Texas at Austin.
Erikson, Kai
  1966. *Wayward Puritans.* New York: Wiley.
Evans-Pritchard, E. E.
  1937. *Witchcraft, Oracles and Magic among the Zande.* Oxford: Clarendon Press.
Firth, Raymond
  1936. *We, the Tikopia.* New York: American Book Co.
Fortes, Meyer
  1969. *Kinship and the Social Order.* Chicago: Aldine.
Foster, George
  1967. *Tzintzuntzan: Mexican Peasants in a Changing World.* Boston: Little, Brown.
Fox, J. Robin
  1967. "Witchcraft and Clanship in Cochiti Therapy." In *Magic, Witchcraft and Curing*, edited by John Middleton. New York: Natural History Press.

Friedson, E.

1965. "Disability as Social Deviance." In *Sociology and Rehabilitation*, edited by Marvin Sussman. Washington, D.C.: American Sociological Association and Vocational Rehabilitation Administration.

Fuente, Julio de la

1949. *Yalalag: Una Villa Zapoteca Serrana.* Serie Científica, no. 1. Mexico City: Museo Nacional de Antropología.

Garretson Selby, Lucy

1972. "The Nature of American Woman: A Cultural Account." Ph.D. dissertation, University of Texas at Austin.

Gearing, Fred

1970. *The Face of the Fox.* Chicago: Aldine.

Glueck, S., and Eleanor T. Glueck

1956. *Unravelling Juvenile Delinquency.* New York: Commonwealth Fund.

Goffman, Erving

1960. *Asylums.* New York: Doubleday.

Goldfrank, Esther

1945. "Socialization, Personality and the Structure of Pueblo Society." In *Personal Character and Cultural Milieu*, edited by D. G. Haring. Rev. ed. Syracuse: Syracuse University Press.

Guiteras-Holmes, C.

1961. *Perils of the Soul: The World View of a Tzotzil Indian.* Glencoe, Ill.: Free Press.

Hallowell, A. Irving

1940. "Aggression in Salteaux Society." *Psychiatry* 13:404–415.

1955. *Culture and Experience.* Philadelphia: University of Pennsylvania Press.

Holland, W.

1961. "Tonalismo y Nagualismo entre los Indios Tzotziles de Larrainzar, Chiapas, Mexico." *Estudios de Cultura Maya* 1.

Hollingshead, August B.

1958. "Factors Associated with the Prevalence of Mental Illness." In *Readings in Social Psychology*, edited by E. E. Maccoby,

T. M. Newcombe, and E. L. Hartley. 3d ed. New York: Holt, Rinehart and Winston.

Hollingshead, August B., and Frederick B. Redlich
　1958.　*Social Class and Mental Illness.* New York: Wiley.

Honigman, John
　1947.　"Witch-fear in post-contact Kaska Society." *American Anthropologist* 49:222–242.

Hotchkiss, John
　1968.　"Children and Conduct in a Ladino Community of Chiapas, Mexico." *American Anthropologist* 69:711–718.

Kaplan, L. H.
　1956.　"Tonal and Nagual in Coastal Oaxaca, Mexico." *Journal of American Folklore* 69.

Kitsuse, John
　1962.　"Societal Reaction to Deviant Behavior: Problems in Theory and Method." *Social Problems* 9:247–256.

Kluckhohn, Clyde
　1944.　*Navaho Witchcraft.* Peabody Museum Papers, vol. 22. Cambridge, Mass.: The Museum.

La Farge, O.
　1947.　*Santa Eulalia: The Religion of a Chuchumatan Indian Town.* Chicago: University of Chicago Press.

La Farge, Oliver, and S. Byers
　1931.　*The Year-Bearer's People.* Middle American Research Series, no. 3. New Orleans: Tulane University.

Leach, E. R.
　1954.　*Political Systems of Highland Burma.* Cambridge, Mass.: Harvard University Press.
　1961.　*Rethinking Anthropology.* London: Athlone Press.

Lemert, Edwin
　1951.　*Social Pathology.* New York: McGraw-Hill.
　1962.　"Paranoia and the Dynamics of Exclusion." *Sociometry* 25:2–25.
　1967.　*Human Deviance, Social Problems and Social Control.* Englewood Cliffs: Prentice-Hall.

Levine, Robert A.
    1962.   "Witchcraft and Co-wife Proximity in Southwestern Kenya."
            Ethnology 11:39–45.
Lévi-Strauss, C.
    1949.   *Les structures élémentaires de la parenté*. Paris: Presses Uni-
            versitaires de France.
    1953.   "Social Structure." In *Anthropology Today*, edited by A. L.
            Kroeber. Chicago: University of Chicago Press.
    1962.   *La pensée sauvage*. Paris: Plon.
    1963.   "The Sorcerer and His Magic." In *Structural Anthropology*,
            translated by Claire Jacobson and Brooke Grudfest Schoepf.
            New York: Basic Books.
Lewis, Oscar
    1951.   *Tepoztlan Revisited: Life in a Mexican Village*. Urbana:
            University of Illinois Press.
    n.d.   "Further Observations on the Folk-Urban Continuum and
            Urbanization with Special Reference to Mexico City."
McCord, William, and Joan McCord
    1959.   *Origins of Crime*. New York: Columbia University Press.
    1960.   *Origins of Alcoholism*. Stanford: Stanford University Press.
Marwick, M. G.
    1952.   "The Social Context of Cewa Witch Beliefs." *Africa* 22:120–
            135; 23:215–233.
Matza, David
    1970.   *Becoming Deviant*. Englewood Cliffs: Prentice-Hall.
Merton, Robert K.
    1957.   *Social Theory and Social Structure*. 2d rev. ed. New York:
            Free Press.
Middleton, John
    1955.   "The Concept of 'Bewitching' in Lugbara." *Africa* 25:252–
            260.
Middleton, John, ed.
    1967.   *Magic, Witchcraft and Curing*. New York: Natural History
            Press.
Morris, T.

1957. *The Criminal Area: A Study in Social Ecology.* London: Routledge and Kegan Paul.

Murray, Henry A.

1938. *Explorations in Personality.* New York: Oxford University Press.

Nadel, Siegfried

1952. "Witchcraft in Four African Societies: An Essay in Comparison." *American Anthropologist* 54:18–29.

Nader, Laura

1964. *Talea and Juquila: A Comparison of Zapotec Social Organization.* Berkeley: University of California Press.

Nash, June

1960. "Social Relations in Amatenango del Valle: An Activity Analysis." Ph.D. dissertation, University of Chicago.

1964. "The Structuring of Social Relations: An Activity Analysis." *Estudios de Cultura Maya* 4:335–359.

Nash, Manning

1958. *Machine Age Maya.* Memoirs of the American Anthropological Association, no. 87. Menasha, Wis.: American Anthropological Association.

1960. "Witchcraft as a Social Process in a Tzeltal Community." *America Indígena* 40:121–126.

Nutini, Hugo

1967. "A Synoptic Comparison of Mesoamerican Marriage and Family Structure." *Southwestern Journal of Anthropology* 23:383–404.

1968. *San Bernadino Contla: Marriage and Family Structure in a Tlaxcalan Municipio.* Pittsburgh: University of Pittsburgh Press.

Oliver, D.

1955. *A Solomon Island Society: Kinship and Leadership among the Siuai of Bougainville.* Cambridge, Mass.: Harvard University Press.

O'Nell, Carl, and H. A. Selby

1968. "Sex Differences in the Incidence of Susto in Two Zapotec

Pueblos: An Analysis of the Relationships between Sex Role Expectation and a Folk Illness." *Ethnology* 7:95–105.

Opler, Morris
  1946. "Chiricahua Apache Material Relating to Sorcery." *Primitive Man* 1:93 and 4:81–92.

Parsons, Elsie Clews
  1936. *Mitla: Town of the Souls*. Chicago: University of Chicago Press.

Rattray, A. S.
  1923. *Ashanti*. Oxford: Clarendon Press.

Reiss, Albert J., and A. L. Rhodes
  1961. "Delinquency and Social Class Structure." *American Sociological Review* 26:720–733.

Richards, Audrey I.
  1935. "A Modern Movement of Witch-Finders." *Africa* 8:448–461.

Romney, A. K.
  1965. "Kalmuk Mongol and the Classification of Lineal Kinship Terminologies." In "Formal Semantic Analysis," edited by E. A. Hammel. *American Anthropologist* 67.

Roy, Donald
  1954. "Efficiency and the 'Fix': Informal Intergroup Relations in a Piecework Machine Shop." *American Journal of Sociology* 60: 255–260.

Rubington, Earl, and Martin S. Weinberg
  1968. *Deviance: The Interactionist Perspective*. New York: Macmillan.

Saler, Benson
  1964. "Nagual, Witch and Sorcerer in a Quiche Village." *Ethnology* 3:305–328.

Scheff, Thomas
  1966. *Being Mentally Ill: A Sociological Theory*. Chicago: Aldine.

Schneider, D. M.
  1968. *American Kinship: A Cultural Account*. Englewood Cliffs: Prentice-Hall.

Schuessler, K. E., and D. Cressey
  1950. "Personality Characteristics of Criminals." *American Journal of Sociology* 55:476–484.
Selby, H. A.
  1966. "Social Structure and Deviant Behavior in a Zapotec Community." Ph.D. dissertation, Stanford University.
Siegel, M.
  1941. "Religion in Western Guatemala: A Product of Acculturation." *American Anthropologist* 43.
Spindler, L.
  1952. "Witchcraft in Menominee Acculturation." *American Anthropologist* 54:393–403.
Szasz, T.
  1961. *The Myth of Mental Illness*. New York: Harper.
Tait, David
  1963. "A Sorcery Hunt in Dagomba." *Africa* 33:136–147.
Taylor, William
  1972. *Landlord and Peasant in Colonial Oaxaca*. Stanford: Stanford University Press.
Villa Rojas, Alfonso
  1963. "El nagualismo como recurso de control social entre los grupos mayances de Chiapas, México." *Estudios de Cultura Maya* 3:243–260.
Wagley, Charles
  1949. *The Social and Religious Life of a Guatemalan Village*. Memoirs of the American Anthropological Association, no. 71. Menasha, Wis.: American Anthropological Association.
Walker, Deward E.
  n.d. "Thoughts on a Collection of Studies Dealing with North American Sorcery." Unpublished manuscript.
  1967. "Nez Perce Sorcery." *Ethnology* 6:66–96.
Whiting, B.
  1950. *Paiute Sorcery*. Viking Fund Publications in Anthropology, no. 15. New York: Wenner Gren Foundation for Anthropological Research.

160 BIBLIOGRAPHY

Wilson, Monica
    1951. "Witch Beliefs and Social Structure." *American Journal of Sociology* 56:307–313.

Wolf, Eric R.
    1955. "Types of Latin American Peasantry." *American Anthropologist* 58:1065–1078.
    1957. "Closed Corporate Peasant Communities in Mesoamerica and Central Java." *Southwestern Journal of Anthropology* 13(1).
    1959. *Sons of the Shaking Earth*. Chicago: University of Chicago Press.

INDEX

abnormality: social nature of, 42–47; varieties of, 48–56

Adam: "sells" wife, 82–83

Adams, R. N.: discusses belief in souls, 99

adultery: with insiders, 75; and matrilocal contract, 73–74, 75; with outsiders, 77–78; for pay, 81–84; sanctions against, 69, 70; and *wana bieha*, 79–81

Alejandra: arranges liaison for husband, 83

Alejandro: abnormality of, 43–46, 47

Allport, Floyd H.: on rumor, 102

Amantenango del Valle: social relations in, 120

Amelia: on abnormal kinship relationship, 47; and alleged witch, 112, 128; on discovery of *tono*, 99; on disease, 105; on identification of witches, 110; identification of witches by, 121, 124; on power of gossip, 124, 126; on suspected infidelity, 90–91; on *tono* death, 104

Ashanti: witchcraft among, 96

Augustino: on discovery of *tono*, 99–100; humility of, 23; marriage arranged by, 73; respectfulness of, 28; restoration of trust by, 26–27; tenure of, as officeholder, 137–138; and would-be borrower, 49

Azande: witchcraft among, 94

Aztecs: and the Conquest, 134

Basso, Keith H., 94; on Western Apache witchcraft, 97–98

Bateson, Gregory, 62

Beattie, John: study of Bunyoro witchcraft by, 94–95

Becker, Howard S.: interactionist analysis of, 9, 10, 11–12

behavior: conscious vs. unconscious models of, 67–68

Bi'či: quarrel of, with neighbor, 48–49, 53; rebellion of, against social games, 54–56

biological theories: as explanation for deviant behavior, 6

Bohannon, Paul: studies West African witchcraft, 95

Boston Strangler: explanation for deviance of, 6

Bunyoro: witchcraft among, 95

Caballo: *tono* of, 99–100

Cambridge-Somerville project, 7

Cameron, N., 12

Carnuto: affair of, with Merina, 101–102

Catarina: affair of, with Ulrico, 83

Cewa: sorcery among, 96

child abandonment: definition of, as deviant behavior, 53–54

child betrothal, 71

child marriage, 71

children: function of, in community,

44; use of witchcraft threats against, 94

Chiricahua Apache: witchcraft among, 94

Church, the: landholdings of, 135–136

čï'up: definition of, as deviant behavior, 53

civil-religious hierarchy: and maintenance of value system, 137–138

climate: importance of, to villagers, 19

closed corporate community: development of, 134, 135, 137; explanation of, 132–134

Cochiti: witchcraft among, 126

compadrazgo: and definition of kinship, 77

Conquest, the: effect of, on Oaxaca Valley, 134–136

Cordry, Donald, 4

Cordry, Dorothy, 4

core witch: defined, 121; place of, in community, 126–127

Cortez, Hernando: indirect rule of, 134

Cressey, D.: on criminal personality, 7

criminal behavior: psychological explanation for, 6–7; social psychological explanation for, 7–8

cuelga: importance of, 127

Dalton, Melville: demonstrates group complicity in deviant behavior, 10

Demeteria: on sense of community, 133–134

Desideria: and witch identification, 121

deviant behavior: hierarchy of, 16, 145–148; modern theories of, 5–14

diet: of villagers, 19

Douglas, Jack D., 21; on definition of deviance, 8–9; on good and evil, 38–39

Douglas, Mary: studies Central African witchcraft, 95

dreams: and identification of witches, 110–111

Durkheim, Émile: on necessity of deviance, 9, 63

Elpidia: death of, 103–104

envy: vs. distance of kinship, 34, 36; nature of, 28–30; and reciprocity, 58–59; social nature of, 107; and witchcraft, 106–107

Erikson, Kai: interactionist analysis of, 11

Eusebia: on behavior of Alejandro, 43, 44; identification of witches by, 120–121, 124; on importance of virginity, 71–72; on judgers, 60–61; on lying, 50; on sexual exploits, 85–86; on wife-selling, 82–83

Evangelina: identified as witch, 112

Evans-Pritchard, E. E.: studies Azande witchcraft, 94

evil: definition of, by society, 40–41; and envy, 29–30; interrelationship of, with good, 13; and kinship relations, 33, 38–39; in Zapotec value system, 21

evil eye: indifference to, 57–59, 60

favors: asking of, as important interaction, 23–25; granting of, as mark of "good man," 28; symbolic significance of, 59–60

fighting: definition of, as deviant behavior, 53

Firth, Raymond: studies Tikopia witchcraft, 96

flag burning: symbolic significance of, 78

Fortes, Meyer: on kinship relations, 140

Foster, George: on limited good, 106

Fox, J. Robin: on Cochiti witchcraft, 126

Fox Indians: social consciousness of, 107–108

Friedson, E.: interactionist analysis of, 11

fright sickness: as form of withdrawal, 52–53

Gearing, Fred: on social consciousness, 107–108